GEARED FOR GROWTH BIBLE STUDIES

ANGELS

A STUDY ON GOD'S SPECIAL AGENTS

BIBLE STUDIES TO IMPACT THE LIVES
OF ORDINARY PEOPLE

Written by Graham M. Trice

The Word Worldwide

WEC
reaching the unreached

CHRISTIAN
FOCUS

For details of our titles visit us on our website
www.christianfocus.com

ISBN 978-1-5271-0310-8

Published in 2018

Christian Focus Publications Ltd.
Geanies House, Fearn, Ross-shire,
IV20 1TW, Scotland, UK
www.christianfocus.com
and
WEC International, The Scala, 115a Far Gosford Street,
Coventry, CV1 5EA, United Kingdom
www.wecinternational.org

Cover design by Daniel van Straaten

Printed by Ashford Colour Press

CONTENTS

QUESTIONS AND NOTES

ANSWER GUIDE

PREFACE

GEARED FOR GROWTH

'Where there's LIFE there's GROWTH:
Where there's GROWTH there's LIFE.'

WHY GROW a group?

Because as we study and share the Bible together we can:

- Learn to combat loneliness, depression, staleness, frustration and other problems
- Get to understand and love one another
- Become responsive to the Holy Spirit's dealing and obedient to God's Word

and that's GROWTH.

HOW do you GROW a group?

- Just start by asking one friend to join you and then aim at expanding your group.
- Study the set portions daily, they are brief and easy: no catches.
- Meet once a week to discuss what you find.
- Befriend others, and work away together

See how it GROWS!

WHEN you GROW ...
Things will happen at school, at home, at work, in your youth group, your student fellowship, women's meetings, midweek meetings, churches, communities and so on.

WHEN you PRAY ...
Remember those involved in the writing and production of these study courses. Pray for groups studying that each member will not only be enriched personally, but will be reaching out continually to involve others. Pray for group leaders and those who direct the studies locally, nationally and internationally.

WHEN you PAY ...
Realise that all profits from the sale of studies go to develop the ministry and have the joy of knowing you are working together with us in the task.

For details of our titles visit us on our websites:
www.christianfocus.com www.gearedforgrowth.co.uk

ISBN 1-84550-020-2 10 9 8 7 6 5 4 3 2 1

INTRODUCTORY STUDY

I treasured the first occasion that I can recollect being called an 'angel' in my childhood. It made such an impact upon me; I felt that I was floating on a cloud! I did not really know much about angels at the time. The person had simply praised me for completing the task they had given me to do. At the time I was inclined to think that the angel Christmas decoration at the top of the Christmas tree was a fairy. It was not until I was converted in my late teens when, as a Christian, I started reading the Bible seriously. It was then that I discovered that angels are God's special messengers. Since then I have never ceased to be amazed by the remarkable accomplishments that are recorded in the Bible and how many times they are mentioned. There are about 280 references.

There is a chart on the next page that lists the names of the Bible books that have at least one reference to an angel or angels.

In preparing these notes I read lots of different books about angels. Many of them were very helpful, and I have listed some of them later that you may like to read. However, it was most unfortunate that all the books on the topic of angels that I borrowed from libraries in my neighbourhood proved to be unhelpful. They were written by authors with highly imaginative minds but they appeared to have virtually ignored what the Bible says about these holy creatures. If you only read one book about angels please make sure that it is the Bible. God has blessed us with His inspired Word, the Bible, which is divided into the Old and New Testament and made up of sixty-six books. Thirty-three of these, which is half the books of the Bible, mention angels, so you can see there is a lot that God wants us to know about His special messengers. Well might the song written by Peter Philip Bilhorn (1865-1936) say, 'Oh, the best book to read is the Bible!'

Have a look through a good hymn book and see if you can find hymns that mention angels. You could start with the Christmas carols, but please look for some others also. I was surprised how many I managed to find.

As we will be reading and thinking about such a variety of different books in the Bible you may find it useful to look at the 'Table of Contents' in the front of the Bible. The books of the Bible are listed and the page number of the first chapter is stated. We shall mostly look at the Old Testament (OT) references to angels first. We will then study the New Testament (NT) which begins with a flurry of angelic activity before thinking about a very special person who has the title the *'Angel of the LORD'* (Gen. 16:7). There are so many helpful lessons to learn about the *'holy angels'* (Matt. 25:31) that we will concentrate on these with just a brief consideration of *'the angels who sinned'* (2 Pet. 2:4).

Before starting the study in detail think about and discuss the questions below.

It would be useful to make some notes at this stage and then you will be able to compare your comments with your views when the series of studies are completed.

- What do you know (or don't know) or believe about angels?
- Have you been able to find some hymns, psalms or spiritual songs that mention angels?
- Have you experienced or do you know anyone who claims to have had an encounter with an angel?
- Do you think encounters with angels are real or imagined?
- How do you expect these Bible studies to help you understand more about angels?

ANGEL(S) – Bible references in New King James Version

OT Books	Occasions
Genesis	15
Exodus	6
Numbers	11
Judges	22
1 Samuel	1
2 Samuel	7
1 Kings	3
2 Kings	3
1 Chronicles	9
2 Chronicles	1
Job	1
Psalms	10
Isaiah	2
Daniel	2
Hosea	1
Zechariah	20

NT Books	Occasions
Matthew	19
Mark	5
Luke	24
John	4
Acts	21
Romans	1
1 Corinthians	4
2 Corinthians	1
Galatians	3
Colossians	1
2 Thessalonians	1
1 Timothy	2
Hebrews	13
1 Peter	2
2 Peter	2
Jude	1
Revelation	76

STUDY 1

I BELIEVE IN ANGELS

QUESTIONS

Day 1 *Psalm 91:9-11; 2 Timothy 3:16-17; Acts17:10-12.*

a) Why is the Bible such a helpful, important, and reliable source for learning about angels?

b) What was so commendable about the people Paul and Silas taught in Berea?

c) When people talk or write about angels what should we be doing?

Day 2 *Luke 15:10; Matthew 4:7-11 & 16:24-27.*

a) Why should we believe in angels?

b) What are the activities of the angels mentioned in today's Gospel readings?

Day 3 *Matthew 16:1-12; Luke 20:27-40; Acts 23:6-10.*

a) Explain how it is possible to be religious, believe in angels and yet not be a Christian?

b) What false teaching did the Sadducees embrace, that is contrary to the Scriptures?

Day 4 *Deuteronomy 29:29; Acts 1:7; Hebrews 1:1-14.*

a) Can we expect our curiosity about angels to be fully satisfied from the Bible?

b) Who is superior to the angels and who requires us to believe in Him?

QUESTIONS (contd)

Day 5 *Hebrews 11:1-3; Colossians 1:13-17; Job 38:1-7.*

a) *'In the beginning God created the heavens and the earth'* (Gen. 1:1) Do you believe this? If so when did you come to believe this? Or, what are your reasons for not believing it?

b) What is the 'hint' in the Bible as to when God created the angels?

Day 6 *Acts 17:22-32; Revelation 19:5-10 & 22:8-9.*

a) Why was the Apostle Paul so concerned for the people of Athens?

b) Why was the angel so concerned by the worship of the Apostle John?

Day 7 *Numbers 22:21-35; John 6:36 & 20:24-31*

a) What had to happen for Balaam to appreciate the presence of the 'Angel of the LORD'?

b) What lesson did Thomas need to learn about seeing and believing?

NOTES

It has become increasingly popular amongst all sorts of people to believe in angels. As I prepared these notes I searched my local council library catalogue using the title key word 'angels'. Over 300 records were found but the only ones I recognised as being based on what the Bible says were those I had donated.

The Swedish music group *Abba* performed a song entitled, 'I have a Dream' in which the line 'I believe in angels' is repeated. Sadly, it is merely about 'a dream' and a 'fairy tale'. What a contrast this is to the statement of G. Campbell Morgan (1863-1945) a former minister of Westminster Chapel in London. Dr Campbell said, 'I believe in the ministry of angels because our Lord taught me to do.'

As a rebellious young teenager I was usually called a 'little devil' because of my outrageous pranks. You can imagine how delighted I was one day when completing a task, to be told by a friend's mother – 'You are an angel!' Some years later, the gospel was explained to me, I was convicted of my sin and trusted in Christ for salvation. When I put my faith in the unseen Saviour I believed that God was my Creator and Redeemer. I soon came to realise I was no angel but I also came to appreciate what is often the unseen ministry of God's special messengers, the angels.

Now over fifty years later, I am so thankful to all the people who have helped me to understand the Bible more clearly. What a joy it has been to discover that angels had an important role first in the Old Testament period and also in Christ's early ministry and the experiences of the Lord's Apostles. Have you noticed from the earlier chart which book in the Bible has the most references to angels? It is the book of Revelation. The Bible informs us about many historical events concerning angels and also many prophetic events.

There are people who do not believe that angels really exist. The Lord Jesus Christ and the Apostles were confronted by such people. A group called the Sadducees did not accept what the Old Testament Scriptures say on the matter. Neither did they believe in the Lord Jesus or the resurrection. Hence such a person was called a 'sad you see'! (Sadducee).

As you go through this study about angels you may well find that questions come to mind. It is worth writing them down as they occur. You may find that some of them are answered in later pages of the study. At other times you will find it helpful to discuss your queries with mature Christians who have a good working knowledge of the Bible. However, we need to remember that God does not always satisfy our idle curiosity. We can be assured of this; all the important things that God wants us to know are recorded in Scripture.

I hope that you will notice as you progress with the study that the angels never seek to draw attention to themselves. They are God's humble and obedient servants. They delight to praise God, do His will, support His people and draw attention to Christ. We can admire the amazing things that they do but we must never worship them. Our adoration must be reserved exclusively for God, who created all things and the eternal Son who alone can save us from judgement.

STUDY 2

'A' IS FOR ANGELS

QUESTIONS

Day 1 **Agents** *Luke 1:26-38; Luke 7:18-28; 2 Corinthians 12:7.*

a) Who was the special messenger sent to Mary and what impact did the message have on her?

b) Who were the messengers who were sent to Jesus and what was their duty?

c) Who was the messenger sent to the Apostle Paul and what was God's purpose for sending him?

Day 2 **Abode** *Mark 13:27, 31-33; Galatians 1:6-8; Revelation 10:1-7.*

a) What is it that the *'angels in heaven'* are ignorant of?

b) What is the Apostle Paul's warning about a possible *'angel from heaven'*?

c) What are the different locations of the angels in John's vision in the Book of Revelation?

Day 3 **Attributes** *Mark 8:34-38; Psalm 103:20; Romans 3:10-23.*

a) What significant characteristics do the angels associated with the Lord Jesus Christ have?

b) What are the contrasting features about the angels in heaven when compared to us on earth?

Day 4 **Appearance** *Genesis 18:1-8; Luke 24:1-8 & 13-23; Numbers 22:20-35.*

a) What evidence is there from Abraham's remarkable experience to show that angels can appear as men?

QUESTIONS (contd)

b) Why was the angel's message to the women at Christ's grave so important?

c) How is it possible for an angel to be nearby and for a person not to realise it?

Day 5 **Activities** *Revelation 4:1-11; Daniel 6:18-23; Acts 12:5-16.*

a) What can we learn from the example of the activities in heaven about how we should worship the Lord while on earth?

b) How were Daniel and Peter greatly encouraged by the intervention of God's angels?

Day 6 **Abundance** *Luke 2:8-16; Hebrews 12:22-24.*

a) What were the shepherds privileged to see and learn from the angels? (Note the number mentioned in Luke 2:13).

b) What are the key words used by the writer of Hebrews that indicate how many angels there are?

Day 7 **Aspiration** *1 Peter 1:3-12; Luke 15:1-10.*

a) What is Peter writing to his Christian readers about that *'angels desire to look into'*?

b) What event on earth causes *'joy in the presence of the angels of God'*?

NOTES

It is probably a rather long time ago, but do you remember being taught the Alphabet? I well remember being told '"A" is for Apple' initially, then gradually I learnt that there were a great deal of other words that also begin with the letter A. For this week's study I have selected words starting with A that will help us in our understanding of what the Bible teaches about angels.

Agents An agent is one who acts and speaks as the representative of another who is superior to them. We sometimes call this person a 'messenger'. This is the word used in the Hebrew Old Testament and also in the Greek New Testament. Sometimes the word is used in the Bible to refer to spiritual beings (angels or demons) but sometimes the word is used of human agents, or messengers. The key feature about such a person is that they have a duty to obey and serve their master.

Abode Most of us quite rightly associate heaven as the place where angels live. However, the Bible tells us a lot about their activities on earth. It is reported of Jacob *'Then he dreamed, and behold, a ladder was set up on the earth, and its top reached to heaven; and there the angels of God were ascending and descending on it'* (Gen. 28:12). This, together with Christ's statement (John 1:21), indicates that the angels move between heaven and earth. They appear to have been issued with a 'return ticket' that permits them to go between worshipping in heaven and working on earth.

Attributes The main abode of God's *'elect angels'* (1 Tim. 5:21), in contrast to the evil ones, is heaven, in the light of God's holy presence. As nothing *'that defiles'* can remain permanently in God's presence (Rev. 21:27) God's angels remain sinless, pure, submissive and obedient. How unlike mankind! However, like us they do have personalities and are held accountable to their Creator. We also know that some of them have names – *Michael* (Jude v. 9) and *Gabriel* (Luke 1:19). A word of warning – if you read about a named angel whose name does not appear in the sixty-six books of the Bible be very suspicious!

Appearance If you admire the magnificent paintings by famous artists, please do not be misled by the way they frequently depict angels in their pictures. When on the rare occasions angels were seen on earth, their appearances are always as real men. They never appear as ghosts, beautiful winged ladies dressed in white robes and certainly not as winged babies or animals. When these *'ministering spirits'* (Heb. 1:14) were seen on earth by Abraham, and others after him, he mistook them for people he had not met before (Heb. 13:2). An angel may not always be visible to us but that does not necessarily mean they are not present. Keep in mind they are *'ministering **spirits**'*.

Activities It has rightly been said that, 'The chief end of man is to glorify God'. It can equally be said of angels that, 'The chief end of the service of angels is the glory of God and the good of humankind'. The main activities of angels in heaven are the worship and adoration of Almighty God – *'let all the angels of God worship Him'* (Heb. 1:6). The main activities of angels on earth are to care for, give protection and offer guidance and encouragement to God's people. Please note carefully the Bible never uses the term 'guardian angel'. The apocryphal book named Tobit (5:4-6 & 12:5) mentions 'Raphael' as the so-called 'guardian angel' but this cannot be regarded as a reliable source. The only two angels named in the 66 inspired books of the Bible are Gabriel and Michael.

Some, wrongly so in my opinion, have taken the words of Christ in Matthew 18:10 to mean that every baby and child has an individual or 'guardian angel' watching over them.

In an old Scottish church there is a frequently quoted inscription that states:

> 'Though God's Power Be Sufficient to Govern Us,
> Yet for Man's Infirmity He appointed His Angels to Watch over Us'

We should be truly thankful for what God has revealed to us about angels in the Bible. Their worship in heaven is a good example to us. Their work on earth ought to be a great encouragement to us if we love the Lord.

Abundance Historically there has been much discussion and speculation about how many angels exist. It is alleged that medieval theologians delighted to debate such matters as, 'How many angels can dance on the head of a pin?' I am tempted to respond by saying, 'It depends how big the pin is!' So much time and energy can be wasted debating matters of no real significance and that they are not taught in the Scriptures.

The terminology used in scripture clearly indicates that the number of angels is vast! Jesus spoke of His Heavenly Father being able to provide ***'more than** twelve legions of angels'* (Matt. 26:53). A Roman legion was made up of 6,500 foot soldiers and those on horseback, thus twelve legions would be 78,000. The Scriptures make it very clear that there is a super abundance of divine messengers who do God's bidding.

Aspiration There is a holy curiosity on the part of the angels to look and learn about the glories of Christ's kingdom in the lives of individual believers from the vantage point of heaven. No Angel, either elect or evil is able to enjoy the blessing of God's grace, mercy and forgiveness. It is an aspiration that will never be a reality for an angel. The death of Christ did not atone for the sins of a single angel. He is the Saviour of multitudes of human sinners who repent and believe on Him, but He is not the Saviour of a single angel. Although they cannot personally experience it *'angels desire to look into'* God's redemptive plan and purpose. The Hymn writer Joseph Swain (1761-1796) writing about the death of Christ on the cross to save sinners said,

> Angels here may gaze and wonder,
> What the God of love could mean
> When He tore that heart asunder,
> Never once defiled with sin.

STUDY 3

WHO'S WHO AMONG THE ANGELS?

QUESTIONS

Day 1 **Evil or Elect?** *John 3:16-21; Jude 5-7.*

a) Who are the two types of people described by the Apostle John, and what are the main differences?

b) What are the consequences for angels and mankind not being faithful to God?

Day 2 **Named Angels** *Revelation 12:7-10; Jude v. 9.*

a) Who was cast out of heaven, along with *'his angels'*?

b) Who was fighting for God and what is his special position?

Day 3 **Unnamed Heavenly Host** *Genesis 2:18-25; Luke 2:13-20; Revelation 5:11-14.*

a) Who did God use to name the earthly creatures He created but not his heavenly host?

b) Who did the Shepherds praise and glorify for what they had seen and heard?

c) What were the unnamed *'many angels'* and the other occupants of heaven doing?

Day 4 **Cherubim** *Genesis 3:17-24; Ezekiel 10:1-19.*

a) What was the first task recorded in the Bible that God gave the cherubim?

b) Bear in mind that the prophet Ezekiel is recording what he saw in a vision, what impresses you most about the role of the silent cherubim?

QUESTIONS (contd)

Day 5 **Seraphim** *Isaiah 6:1-7.*

a) What was the message and ministry of the Seraphim that Isaiah the prophet saw?

b) How many wings do these angelic creatures have and how does this compare with pictures of angels that you have seen?

c) What is one of the main differences between the activities of Cherubim and Seraphim?

Day 6 **Sons of God** *Genesis 6:1-8; Job 1:6-12; Romans 8:1-17.*

Taking into consideration what Jesus said about angels and procreation (Mark 12:25), who are the *'sons of God'* in the following Bible references?

a) Genesis 6:2.

b) Job 1:6 & 2:1.

c) Romans 8:14.

Day 7 **Ministering Spirits** *Hebrews 1:13-14; Psalm 91:11-12.*

a) A Christian author, referring to angels, has exclaimed, 'The courtiers of heaven ministering to the worms of the earth!' If *you* are a Christian, how does it make you feel that God has His mighty angels serving *you*?

b) Can *you* name a godly person in the Old Testament and another in the New Testament who experienced the protective ministry of angels? Please write the Bible references down.

NOTES

This week's theme is 'Who's Who amongst the angels?' We will consider just some of the many names and classifications of the created spiritual beings, collectively known as 'angels'.

Evil or Elect? God has placed us on this earth in which there is such vast diversity. A group of scientists have estimated that there are roughly 8.7 million different species on our planet (that is give or take 1.3 million). How amazing that there are basically only two types of people in God's sight – the converted and the unconverted. The same is true of the *'an innumerable company'* (Heb. 12:22) of angels – they are either faithful or they are fallen, they are elect or they are evil, there are the devoted and the demonic. In case you want an answer to the frequently asked question, 'Who created the Devil?' please be patient, I will give the answer in a later study.

Named Angels The challenge that every teacher is confronted with as they face a new class of students is the task of naming each child. The church minister has a similar job naming all the people in a new congregation. We are spared from having a long list of the personal names of angels in the Bible. There are only three. There is the fallen angel we know as *'Lucifer'* (Isa. 14:12) which means 'shining one' or 'star of the morning'. He is also commonly known as *'the Devil and Satan'* (Rev. 12:9).

There are two named faithful angelic messengers of God, Michael and Gabriel. All other angel names, and there are several of them, are not found in the Bible. Michael's name means, 'Who is like God?' He is the only named angel with the special title archangel (Jude v. 9). Gabriel's name means, 'Mighty One of God'. Note that he appeared both in the time of Daniel (6th century B.C.) and at the time of Christ's incarnation.

Unnamed Heavenly Host The Psalmist has this wonderful reassurance for those who love the Lord, *'The LORD of hosts is with us'* (Ps. 46:7 & 11). This frequently used Old Testament title of God indicates that He is the eternal creator of all things. God maintains the whole of His creation and every person and being is under His dominion. This includes the *'hosts'* of both heaven and earth (Gen. 2:1; Isa. 45:12).

It may well be that God wants the vast *'multitude of heavenly host'* to remain anonymous. Anonymous donors want to help but do not want to be personally thanked and praised; this may also be true of angels.

Cherubim In the Bible these are creatures, *not* cute-looking, naked, chubby babies with wings! We have a limited knowledge of their role. They appear to have been created with a majestic appearance, tremendous power and they assert divinely given authority. They are first mentioned in Genesis 3:24. These winged creatures are closely associated with God's awesome presence. Images of cherubim were in the tabernacle, during the time of Moses (Exod. 25:19-20 & 26:1) and also in the temple built by King Solomon (1 Kings 6:23-35). Remarkably, Satan was once *'the anointed cherub'*, until he sinned against God (Ezek. 28:14-15).

They are mentioned most frequently in the book of Ezekiel where they are seen by the prophet in a series of visions. A notable feature about them is that they are normally the silent servants of God. There is no record in Scripture of the faithful cherubim uttering a single word, but they silently proclaim God's holiness and authority.

Seraphim The Hebrew word means 'burning ones'. Like the cherubim they have a close association with God's glorious presence in heaven. They do not appear on earth and are only seen in visions. The *'living creatures'* mentioned in the Book of Revelation resemble them closely (e.g. see Revelation chapters 4 and 5).

Sons of God When studying the Bible care has to be taken. A single verse must be understood in the context of the chapter, book and the rest of the Bible. If this is not done confusion and misinterpretation will arise. The phrase *'sons of God'* occurs about ten times in the Bible. It is the context in which it is used, together with other relevant verses that will help you to understand who it is referring to. The phrase *'sons of God'* is used mostly of God's holy people – *'... you are all* ***sons of God*** *through faith in Christ Jesus'* (Gal. 3:26). However, there are other occasions when this title is attributed to angels. Keep in mind what Christ said about angels. In Mark 12:25, they do not engage in procreation.

Ministering Spirits While angels sometimes reveal themselves for a limited period in the form of human bodies they are described as *'spirits'* (Heb. 1:14). They do not get married (Matt. 22:30) and neither do they suffer death as we do (Luke 20:36). God created them to minister, that is to serve. They serve God, their Eternal Creator and also the people of God on earth, for whom He is concerned. Hence, when these normally unseen servants appear on earth, they frequently do so to especially be of assistance to those who are trusting in the Lord.

STUDY 4

FEATURES OF ANGELS WHO HAVE FALLEN

QUESTIONS

Day 1 **Satan's Origin** *Isaiah 14:12-15; Ezekiel 28:11-15 & 17; I Corinthians 10:11-13.*

a) What was the ambition of *'Lucifer'* (the Day Star)? Note the reoccurrence of the phrase *'I will'.*

b) How did God respond to such grand schemes?

c) How can the lamentation for the *'King of Tyre'* serve as a warning to us?

Day 2 **Individuals Influenced by Satan** *Genesis 3:1-24; Romans 5:18-19; Luke 22:1-6 & 31-34.*

a) How did Satan's first activity on earth ruin all human relationships with God?

b) How does Satan's influence over Judas and Peter differ and affect the outcome in their lives?

Day 3 **Satan versus the Saviour** *Matthew 4:1-11; Mark 8:27-38.*

a) What do you consider to be particularly subtle about Satan's approach to Jesus?

b) How did Jesus respond to each of Satan's temptation and overcome them?

c) Why did the Saviour rebuke Peter so sternly and who prompted his statement?

Day 4 **The Wicked One and the Word of God** *Genesis 3:1-5; Matthew 13:18-23 & 34-43; I Thessalonians 2:13-18.*

a) How was the subtle serpent undermining the truth and authority of God's Word in the Garden of Eden?

QUESTIONS (contd)

b) What are the two things Satan (*'the wicked one'*) does to hinder the Word of God and the extension of Christ's kingdom?

c) Why might Satan want to hinder the ministry of the Apostle Paul?

Day 5 **The Ferocious Foe** *I Peter 5:8-9; Ephesians 6:10-20; James 4:7.*

a) What does the Apostle Peter tell us to do in order to avoid being devoured by our ferocious foe?

b) Why is it so important for Christians to comply with all the Apostle Paul's instructions about standing against the Devil's schemes?

c) What is your reaction to James' instruction and reassurance?

Day 6 **A Murderer and a Liar** *John 8:37-47; Acts 5:1-11.*

a) How is it possible for many to know and talk about Jesus but not have God as their heavenly Father? Note Christ's words in John 8:42 & 47.

b) Who influenced Ananias to lie and what was the sad outcome?

Day 7 **Satan's Present Limitation and Future Condemnation** *Mark 1:21-28; John 12:28-33, Mark 15:33-39.*

a) What do the questions uttered by the unclean (evil) spirit reveal about demons?

b) What has the Lord Jesus Christ done that has limited the power of the *'prince/ruler of this world'*, Satan?

NOTES

Many years ago a kind friend, sensing my need, presented me with a dictionary. I was surprised to find that it was a 'Dictionary of Synonyms and Antonyms'. Until then I had not really thought much about the need to know about words with a similar or opposite meaning. It was only when I became a Christian that I was made aware of opposites in the spiritual realm. When asked to think about the opposite to God, I guess most people would say, 'Satan' or 'the Devil'. Sadly, so many people do not know what the Bible teaches about these two opposites. The Apostle Paul writing to Christians said, *'we are not ignorant of his devices'* (2 Cor. 2:11). In this week's study we will learn about the origin, some characteristic features and also of the final condemnation of the worst foe of God and Christians.

Satan's Origin When He created the universe, *'God saw everything that He had made, and indeed it was very good'* (Gen. 1:31). Then *'by one man's disobedience many were made sinners'* (Rom. 5:19). Disobedience to God always has horrendous consequences both on earth and in heaven.

Many scholars agree that much of the lamentation for *'the King of Tyre'* applies to Satan (Ezek. 28:1-17). God created a holy and beautiful cherubim who held a special position among the angels as *'the anointed cherub'* (Ezek. 28:14). The sin of pride was his downfall as he desired to exalt himself. The Lord Jesus Christ said, *'I saw Satan fall like lightning from heaven'* (Luke 10:18). He who once dwelt in the light of God's glorious presence will be cast *'into the everlasting fire prepared for the devil and his angels'* (Matt. 25:41). Just as the Saviour has His devoted followers, Satan has his deluded followers. There is but one Devil but there are many demons.

Individuals Influenced by Satan Having fallen from heaven, Satan was quick to influence people living on earth – Adam and Eve (Gen. 3). While Satan has been granted temporary access to heaven his main activities take place on earth. Job 1:6-7 & 2:1-2 inform us about Satan's speeches before the angels in heaven and his scrutiny of people on the earth. He appears to take a personal interest in people, especially the Lord Jesus Christ and those who, by God's grace, have been rescued from Satan's kingdom.

Satan versus the Saviour During the time of Jesus's infancy Satan would have been pleased to have eradicated the Saviour. Through an angelic intervention Jesus and his family escaped the evil plan of King Herod to kill Him (Matt. 2:13). Then as soon as the Lord began His public ministry the Devil commenced his vicious threefold attack on Him (Matt. 4:1-11). Satan did not want to be crushed at Calvary, as predicted by God in the Garden of Eden (Gen. 3:15). He did not want Jesus to suffer on the cross that He might *'save His people from their sins'* (Matt. 1:21).

The Wicked One and the Word of God We need to bear in mind that the meaning of some words change with the passing of time and others take on a double meaning. When a young person today exclaims that their birthday party was 'Wicked!' they mean that they had a really great time. This is not the way the word is used in the Bible. In the Scriptures it denotes evil. The Apostle Paul, writing to Christians reminded them that they had heard *'the* *word of truth, the gospel ...'* (Eph. 1:13). Satan hates the truth and he will do all he can to spread wicked lies about God and His Word. He will even transform *'himself into an angel of light'* in his efforts to deceive people.

The Ferocious Foe I was often asked, 'What do you want to do when you leave school?' I never thought of answering, 'I want to be a lion tamer!' When I enquired about joining the army, I did not realise how dangerous that could be. We should never underestimate the strength of an enemy, it could be disastrous. Jesus asked, *'What king, going to make war against another king, does not sit down first and consider whether he is able with ten thousand to meet him who comes against him with twenty thousand?'* (Luke 14:31). The Apostle Paul describes the enemy of our souls as, *'the prince of the power of the air'* (Eph. 2:2). As Christians, while remembering that Satan is a ferocious foe, we must also keep in mind that the Saviour is a faithful friend. He will never leave us or forsake us (Heb. 13:5) as we do battle with this hungry, ferocious *'roaring lion'* (1 Pet. 5:8). Isaac Watts [1674-1748] succinctly wrote in a hymn:

Should all the hosts of death,
And powers of hell unknown,
Put their most dreadful forms
Of rage and malice on,
I shall be safe; for Christ displays
Superior power and guardian grace.

A Murderer and a Liar King David was guilty of being a murderer and a liar. However, when he was confronted and convicted of his terrible deeds, he sincerely repented and God, in His mercy, forgave him (2 Sam. 11-12; Ps. 51). The Ten Commandments (Exod. 20:13 & 16), together with the teaching of the Lord Jesus Christ clearly forbid such sins. Satan, unlike David, will not cease from engaging in these abominable offences that are the exact opposite of what our Holy God has commanded.

Satan's Present Limitation and Future Condemnation If I had done something seriously wrong as a child I would shudder on hearing the threat, 'You just wait till your father gets home!' I expected to be punished but I did not know when. Satan was told in the Garden of Eden that Christ, *'the seed of the woman'* would bruise his head (Gen. 3:15). Satan suffered a crushing blow at Calvary as Christ bound the *'strong man'* (Mark 3:27). He *'disarmed principalities and powers ... triumphing over them'* (Col. 2:15). While seeking to slow the extension of Christ's kingdom, Satan cannot stop the spread of the gospel. He is still powerful but God remains Almighty! People are now being redeemed *'Out of every tribe and tongue and people and nation'* (Rev. 5:9). Satan, together with his legions of demons, are waiting in anticipation of experiencing God's wrath and final judgement (Rev. 20:10).

STUDY 5

THE SAVIOUR'S SUPREMACY OVER ANGELS

QUESTIONS

Day 1 **Confusion over Christ** *Luke 9:18-20 & 22:66-71; John 20:11-18.*

a) How did the opinions of the crowds differ to Peter's understanding of Christ?

b) What do Christ's replies, to the Jewish council's demand for information, reveal about Himself?

c) Having seen two angels, Mary was momentarily confused about the risen Saviour. How was she made to realise her initial mistaken identification?

Day 2 **Christ and Angels Contrasted – Seated or Surrounding the Throne** *Hebrews 1:1-3 & 13; 8:1-2; Revelation 3:19-22.*

a) What did Christ do on earth before He, *'sat down at the right hand of the Majesty on high'*?

b) What is implied by God not inviting any of the angels to *'Sit at My right hand'*?

c) What is Christ's amazing promise, never made to angels, but to the Christians *'who overcome'*?

Day 3 **Christ and Angels Contrasted – The name above all names** *Matthew 1:18-21; Hebrews 1:1-4; Philippians 2:5-10.*

a) Why was the incarnate Son of God given the name *'JESUS'*?

b) Why is Christ honoured with a *'more excellent name'* than angels?

c) Why will *'every knee'* one day bow *'at the name of Jesus'*?

Day 4 **Christ and Angels Contrasted – The Majestic Son and the Ministering Spirits** *Psalm 2:1-12; Psalm 104:1-4; Hebrews 1:5, 7 & 14.*

a) How do today's Bible readings in the Psalms show that the eternal Son of God is majestic and superior to the angels?

QUESTIONS (contd)

b) Where are the Old Testament quotations taken from in today's Bible reading that show the contrast between Christ and the angels? (You may find a 'Reference Bible' useful.)

Day 5 Christ and Angels Contrasted – Requiring or Refusing Worship
Psalm 148:1-5; Hebrews 1:6; Revelation 22:8-9.

a) Why are *'His angels'*, and the heavenly host, told to *'praise the LORD!'* by the Psalmist?

b) What is the command given to *'the angels of God'* that also applies to each of us?

c) What were the angel's negative and positive instructions to the Apostle John?

Day 6 Christ and Angels Contrasted – The Creator who does not change
Hebrews 1:8-12 & 13:8; Malachi 3:6(a).

a) What are the implications of the *'Son'* having a throne that is eternal, being addressed as *'God'*, having a sceptre and a kingdom?

b) As you live in a constantly changing world, what is your reaction to the declaration of the LORD recorded in Malachi?

Day 7 Christ and Angels Contrasted – Jesus, 'a little lower than the angels'?
Psalm 8:3-8; Hebrews 2:5-9.

a) Charles Darwin described man as 'an efficient animal'. How does Darwin's opinion differ from David's inspired comments about mankind in Psalm 8?

b) How is the humiliation and exaltation of Christ referred to by the writer of Hebrews?

NOTES

In 1975 Dr Billy Graham wrote 'When I decided to preach a sermon on angels, I found practically nothing in my library'. In recent years there has been a huge surge of interest in angels. The secular press has novels, there are cults and occult publications about angels, the new age movement and others have expressed their interest in the topic. The novelty of trying to find out the name of your 'Guardian Angel' is gaining interest. Some non-Christians have started to idolise angels rather than trusting in the Lord. The Apostle Paul wrote of people exchanging *'the truth of God for the lie, and worshiped and served the creature rather than the Creator'* (Rom. 1:25). The unnamed human author of the Book of Hebrews began his letter by writing about the supremacy of Christ over angels. This was because his original readers had apparently become preoccupied with angels and failed to appreciate the supremacy of Christ. Today we need to beware of those claiming that Christ was an angel. He is their Creator and therefore has supremacy over them. This is the theme for this week's study.

Confusion about Christ and Angels We can be easily confused about a multitude of complexities in our time. Many have been confused in the past as well as the present about the Lord Jesus Christ. This is a matter of the greatest importance. If we have come to a right understanding of who Christ is it is because God has revealed it (Matt. 16:17; 1 Cor. 10:10-11). We will then long for the day when the crowds *'confess that Jesus Christ is Lord, to the glory of God the Father'* (Phil. 2:11).

Christ and Angels Contrasted – Seated or Surrounding the Throne During the Old Testament period there were two special constructions where the people of God worshipped and the priests served. Both the Tabernacle and the Temple had angelic creatures displayed in the form of cherubim, but neither of them had any provision for the priest to sit down. This symbolised the fact that their work was required continuously. What a contrast to the Great High Priest and King, the Lord Jesus Christ. When He had finished His work of providing a means of salvation for all who repent and believe in Him, He *'sat down at the right hand of the throne of God'* (Heb. 12:2). Now seated in heaven, the Lord is surrounded by the praising occupants of heaven (Rev. 5:11 & 7:11). Note: it is Christ who has the honour and authority to be seated, while the angels and others surround the throne worshipping.

Christ and Angels Contrasted – The name above all names In the book of Hebrews the writer rightly insists that Christ is *'so much better than the angels'* (Heb. 1:4). This serves both as a reminder to true believers and a rebuke to those who have yet to realise the divinity of the Saviour. The human author of Hebrews does not want to deride the importance and significance of angels. However, it is important that we are fully persuaded of the superiority of Christ. This is because there is no *'salvation in any other, for there is no other name under heaven given among men by which we must be saved'* (Acts 4:12).

Christ and Angels Contrasted – The Majestic Son and the Ministering Spirits *'Son of God'* and *'Son of Man'* are both interchangeable titles ascribed to the Lord Jesus Christ. The first of these titles indicates His divinity, He is eternally God. The second title affirms

His humanity, He *'became flesh and dwelt among us'* (John 1:14). Christ, the majestic Son of Man, came to this earth with a specific mission to accomplish. He came to save sinners who repent and believe in Him by dying on the cross as their substitute. *'... the Son of Man did not come to be served, but to serve, and to give His life a ransom for many'* (Mark 10:45). By way of contrast, the angels are sent to serve; they are God's *'ministering spirits'.* They serve the *'saints'* (God's people) but unlike the majestic Son they can never save sinners.

Christ and Angels Contrasted – Requiring or Refusing Worship In the time of Moses God complained about the Israelites. He had delivered them from the false worship in Egypt and given them the Ten Commandments to guide them. God said, *'They have turned aside quickly out of the way which I commanded them. They have made themselves a molten calf, and worshiped it ...'* (Exod. 32:8). A problem arose in the early Christian church. Some were *'turning aside'* from God's Word that requires us to worship God alone. This is likely to happen when created things, including angels, are revered more than the divine Creator of all things. It is a sad fact that the errors of the past are often repeated in the present.

Christ and Angels Contrasted – The Creator who does not change The Apostle John states that Christ, the eternal Word, created all things (John 1:1-3). This included the angels. Likewise the Apostle Paul, speaking of the eternal Son of God declares, *'by Him all things were created that are in heaven and that are on earth, visible and invisible, whether thrones or dominions or principalities or powers. All things were created through Him and for Him. And He is before all things, and in Him all things consist'* (Col. 1:16-17). As there is no procreation amongst the angels (Mark 12:25) and as they did not evolve, they must have been individually created by God. While the elect angels do not perish, they are not eternal, they had a beginning. While all angels were without sin in their original state, Satan and his angels rebelled and became evil. There was a radical change for the worse among some of the angels but their Creator affirms, *'I am the LORD, I do not change'* (Mal. 3:6).

Christ and Angels Contrasted – Jesus, *'a little lower than the angels'*? Having considered the Biblical evidence that shows that Christ is Superior to God's special agents the angels, it may sound strange to read that Jesus *'was made a little lower than the angels'* (Heb. 2:9). This was for a special reason and for a limited season. When the incarnate Son came to earth He did so in order to be, like all mankind, subject to death. Thus He became *'a little lower than the angels'.* This contrasts with angels who do not die (Luke 20:36).

While the statement applies to the dignity of mankind it also relates to the humanity of the Messiah. Following His crucifixion and resurrection Jesus appeared to His disciples in a glorified body that could be seen and touched (John 20:27). He then ascended into heaven with a visible body (Acts 1:9-11). Angels, who are normally invisible spirits, sometimes appearing in the form of men to accomplish the mission that God had sent them on (Gen. 19:1-2). They remain essentially *'spirits'* (Heb. 1:14) in submission to their Creator and are fully accountable (1 Cor. 6:3).

STUDY 6

ANGELIC APPEARANCES AND APPOINTMENTS

QUESTIONS

Day 1 **Lot – Fleeing from the Fire** *Genesis 19:1-29; Luke 17:26-30.*

a) Why was the angels' message for Lot and his family so urgent?

b) How did the *'two angels'* both punish the evil men and also protect the godly in Sodom?

c) Why did Christ use the illustration of Lot and Sodom during His earthly ministry?

Day 2 **Abraham – The Intervention that Saved Isaac**
Genesis 22:1-19; Hebrews 11:8-12 & 17-19.

a) How did the intervention of the Angel of the Lord affect Abraham and God's promise to him?

b) What impresses you most about the timing of the Angel's instruction to Abraham?

Day 3 **Eliezer – Locating a Beautiful Bride**
Genesis 24:1-21, 37-41 & 50-67; Proverbs 18:22.

a) How did God's help in the past stimulate Abraham's confidence in locating a bride for his son Isaac? See Genesis 24:7.

b) What did Abraham's servant do before speaking to Rebekah when she came to the well?

Day 4 **David – The Plague that Produced Penitence**
2 Samuel 24:10-25; 2 Corinthians 7:9-10; Hebrews 12:5-11.

a) What was David's reaction when he saw the angel striking the people?

b) Having admitted his sin, what else did the Lord require David to do?

QUESTIONS (contd)

c) Even though the Lord loves His people what does He sometimes have to do?

Day 5 Elijah – Strengthen for Service

I Kings 19:1-8; Genesis 3:17-18; 2 Thessalonians 3:10.

a) What happened to make Elijah so fearful?

b) What effect did the food prepared and provided by the angel have on the Lord's prophet?

c) Normally it is not an angel who provides us with food, how does it usually happen?

Day 6 Isaiah – The Seraphim's Repetition and Reassurance

Isaiah 6:1-8; Hebrews 12:14.

a) What are the seraphim in heaven preoccupied with calling to each other?

b) What was the important task done and message given to Isaiah by the seraphim?

c) Why is personal holiness so important to each of us?

Day 7 Daniel – Deliverance from the Lion's Den

Daniel 6:10-23; Hebrews 11:32-34.

a) Despite his anxiety, how did King Darius express his confidence that Daniel would be delivered from the lions?

b) How did Daniel explain his deliverance to the king?

c) Why had Daniel not even been injured by the lions (v. 23)?

NOTES

Herbert Lockyer has stated: 'The chief end of the service of angels is the glory of God and the good of humankind.'[1] This fact is seen repeatedly throughout the whole of the Bible starting from Genesis. In this study we consider seven men who lived during the period of the Old Testament, that is prior to Christ's incarnation. They were all privileged to experience some remarkable and very personal appointments with God's special agents.

Lot – Fleeing from the Fire The Apostle Peter recalls how God brought death and destruction upon the ungodly in the cities of Sodom and Gomorrah. Simultaneously, by the intervention of angels, He *'delivered righteous Lot, who was oppressed by the filthy conduct of the wicked'* (2 Pet. 2:6-9). Note how the angels are referred to as *'men'* by the perverted citizens of Sodom (Gen. 19:5). There is no indication that they were winged, harp-playing, halo-endowed beings that float around on clouds! The Lord Jesus Christ used the event as a powerful warning and illustration.

The Hymn writer, Isaac Watts (1674-1748), referring to the twin roles of the Lord's angels has said,

'Before His feet their armies wait,
And swift as flames of fire they move
To manage His affairs of state,
In works of vengeance or of love'.

Abraham – The Intervention that Saved Isaac My stepmother claimed that she saved me from the flames of a grass fire that I had mischievously started in my childhood. However, that rescue plan fades into insignificance compared with the angelic intervention in the lives of Abraham and his son Isaac. They had the fire and the wood, but what they needed was a lamb. God was testing the faith of His Patriarch in an unusual way. The godly Puritan Thomas Watson wrote, 'God is to be trusted when His providences seem to run contrary to His promises'. The angelic intervention had an immediate impact on that one family. In the future it was to also make an impact upon multitudes of people, as God provided *'the Lamb of God who takes away the sin of the world'* (John 1:29).

Eliezer – Locating a Beautiful Bride The idiom, 'A marriage made in heaven' is used to describe a couple who enjoy a very happy marriage relationship together. In the case of Isaac and Rebekah it really was true. The servant Eliezer was sent on a special mission by his master Abraham. Eliezer was to bring back a bride from a godly family for his son Isaac. He was not to marry a pagan Canaanite. This was an 'arranged marriage' that had the assistance of an angel (Gen. 24:7 & 40). There was an air of confidence that the Lord would both guide and provide the needed *'virtuous wife'.*

David – The Plague that Produced Penitence It has well been said that we should be careful about what we pray for. David, the King of Israel once prayed for enemies who were

1. **All the Angels of the Bible**, Herbert Lockyer, Hendrickson Publishers, seventh printing 2012, ISBN 978-1-59563-198-4

seeking to kill him. He said to Almighty God, *'Let them be like chaff before the wind, and let the angel of the LORD chase them. Let their way be dark and slippery, and let the angel of the LORD pursue them'* (Ps. 35:5-6). I cannot imagine that David ever expected that instead of his people being delivered by an angel, they would be destroyed at the hand of one. This passage is one of those rare events when an angel is seen striking God's people because of their sin. Even in His wrath on this occasion God remembered mercy (Hab. 3:2). This was not so much an act of complete condemnation by God as His chastising. David appears to have had more confidence in the size of the army than he had in the strength of the Lord. He needed to be convinced of the seriousness of his sin.

Elijah – Strengthened for Service Depression is a very debilitating affliction that is no respecter of persons. Godly people have been in oppressive circumstances and at times been caused to ask, 'Why?' In two Psalms the writer asks himself, *'Why are you cast down, O my soul?'* He then encourages himself saying, *'Hope in God'* (Ps. 42:11 & 43:5). The mental health condition of depression has been described as, 'living in a body that fights to survive, with a mind that tries to die.' Elijah the prophet was going through a really rough time. He felt suicidal and there was no anti-depressant medication available to help him. However, he was provided with some amazing food – 'Angel Delight'! Elijah had a long journey and another important task ahead of him. The angel provided him with the much needed sustenance.

Isaiah – The Seraphim's Repetition and Reassurance Moses asked some rhetorical questions, *'Who is like You, O LORD, among the gods? Who is like You, glorious in holiness, fearful in praises, doing wonders?'* (Exod. 15:11). Anyone who has had a close personal encounter with the Lord is made intensely aware of God's greatness and holiness. This was true for the prophet Isaiah when, in a vision, he was granted a glimpse of the Lord enthroned in heaven. It is the only instance in the Bible where we read about *'seraphim'.* These 'fiery beings' are a special class among the angels who never appear on earth with their six wings; see Study 3, Day 5. They are seen praising God and preparing God's prophet for service.

Daniel – Deliverance from the Lion's Den If you have ever attended a Sunday school class as a child there is a very strong possibility that you were told about Daniel and the den of lions. On being told to draw a picture of the event one child in the class drew Daniel surrounded by lions with muzzles on! Personally, I do not blame the child for getting it wrong, but the teacher who failed to fully inform the children of what really happened. Neither was Daniel's deliverance due to the lions being tame or not hungry. The gruesome details of Daniel 6:24 clearly reveal the contrary.

It was nothing less than an amazing divine intervention in which an angel was appointed to shut the lions' mouths. Clearly Daniel was a man whose faith was firmly in the Lord. Daniel is not named in the 'Great Faith Chapter' of the Bible, Hebrews 11 but verse 23 concludes with a strong implication.

STUDY 7

THE ANGEL WHO IS ALMIGHTY

QUESTIONS

Day 1 **Hagar – Help for the Homeless** *Genesis 16:7-14 & 21:1-21.*

a) What does the statement the *'Angel of the LORD found her'* (Gen. 16:7) signify?

b) What is it about how the Angel of the LORD and Hagar spoke to each other that indicates that this was no ordinary created angel?

Day 2 **Jacob – The Wrestler with a Weakness**
Genesis 32:22-32; 2 Corinthians 12:9; Revelation 22:1-5.

a) What statements in Genesis 32 indicate that the Angel Jacob wrestled with was no mere man?

b) How did the physical infirmities of both Jacob and Paul help these godly men?

c) Who are being referred to in the statement, *'they shall see His face'* (Rev. 22:4)?

Day 3 **Moses – Motivated for a Mission** *Exodus 2:11-25 - 3:1-12.*

a) What were Moses' responsibilities before and after the *'Angel of the LORD'* appeared to him?

b) What had God observed about His needy people in Egypt that led to Moses being motivated to go back to the country he had fled from?

Day 4 **Balaam – Blindness that was Banished**
Numbers 22:21-35; Psalm 25:11; Matthew 7:21-23.

a) What two things did the Lord *'open'* and how did it help in the situation?

b) Balaam told the *'Angel of the LORD', 'I have sinned'* but he never asked to be pardoned – why is this so significant?

QUESTIONS (contd)

c) What do you consider to be the chief issue we need to remember in view of Balaam's activities and what Jesus taught?

Day 5 **Joshua – Directives about Demolition**
Exodus 23:20-24; Joshua 5:13 - 6:1-5; Hebrews 11:30.

a) What was Joshua, like Moses (Exod. 3:5) told to do in recognition that He was in the holy presence of God?

b) Why would God's directives to Joshua and the Israelites have been so challenging for them to fully comply with?

Day 6 **Manoah – A Son named Samson** *Judges 13:1-25.*

a) How many times does the title the *'Angel of the LORD'* occur in this chapter and how is He described in verse 6?

b) What caused Manoah and his wife to think they would die as a result of having seen the person they had previously called 'A Man of God'?

Day 7 **Elijah – Commissioned and Consoled**
2 Kings 1:1-18; Deuteronomy 18:22; Matthew 28:16-20.

a) What did Elijah do in response to the Angel's command (v. 3) and reassurance (v. 15)?

b) How was Elijah attested to be a true prophet of God?

c) Who was originally also told to *'Go'* by Jesus Christ?

NOTES

In the course of preparing this study I discovered a word I had not known before. 'Orthography' – the art of writing words with the proper letters according to **standard usage**. It strikes me that when sending a text message from a mobile phone the 'standard use' of many is to use mostly lower case letters. This includes the personal pronoun 'I' that is written as 'i'. I have also been informed that if you use all CAPITAL LETTERS it symbolises shouting, which can be rude and offensive. When we turn to the Bible there is a **standard usage** of capital letters. Hence, in Genesis 1:1 the eternal creator of all things is called God; spelt with a capital G. Man-made gods are written with the first letter in lower case. Note the example of Psalm 95:3 *'For the LORD is the great God, and the great King above all gods'.* Even the word 'LORD' is capitalised. This follows the tradition of the King James Authorised Version when the covenant name of God is translated into English.

This is a helpful feature for when we are studying angels and reading our English translation of the Bible. There are over fifty references in the Old Testament to a person called the 'Angel of the LORD'. Note carefully the use of the capital first letter in the word 'Angel' and the use of all capital letters in the use of the *'LORD'.* This Bible orthography will assist our study this week. It makes it easier to recognise the appearances of the Lord Jesus Christ as the *'Angel of the LORD'.* These were pre-incarnate appearances of the eternal Son of God on earth before the virgin birth in Bethlehem. He is described as an Angel but unlike all other angels, He is Almighty. It is as if God is expressing His earnest desire to be with His people. In this study we will consider the experience of several different people who were visited by the Angel who is Almighty and we shall begin with a lady.

Hagar – Help for the Homeless Poor Hagar, she really was treated badly by her mistress Sarai, later renamed Sarah (Gen. 17:15). Before Sarah had a son, Isaac, she was most unkind to Hagar (Gen. 16) making her homeless. Sarah did it again after her son Isaac was born (Gen. 21). In each instance Hagar was made homeless. On both occasions it was the *'Angel of the LORD' / 'the angel of God'* who instructed, reassured and predicted a favourable outcome. Writers use the word 'Theophany' when referring to such divine visible manifestations. Hagar's experience is the first one recorded in the Scriptures.

Jacob – The Wrestler with a Weakness When angels appeared to people on earth they frequently appeared in the recognisable form of men. When God's special agents visited Abraham he viewed the angels as *'three men standing in front of him'* (Gen. 18:2). When referring to the person that Jacob had his night time encounter with, we are told *'a **Man** wrestled with him until the breaking of day'.* (Note the use of the capital letters in the passage). While the phrase *'the Angel of the LORD'* does not occur in this passage, Hosea 12:3-4 informs us that Jacob *'struggled with the Angel'.* There is much to indicate that this is a 'Theophany'. The purpose of the physical contest between the divine visitor and Jacob was designed to make a spiritual impact on him. It was God who had changed Jacob's grandparents names (Gen. 17:5 & 15). Now God changed His name and this wrestling experience transformed Jacob's character. He is no longer the cunning deceiver but one who was contrite and devoted to the Lord. The Apostle Paul also suffered a physical affliction for his spiritual good.

Moses – Motivated for a Mission The appearance of *'the Angel of the LORD'* to Moses, rather like the experience of Hagar and Jacob, took place in an isolated location. It is as if

God has to get some people away from the distractions of the world so as to get their full attention. Notice it was not Moses who commended himself for the task (2 Cor. 10:18), in fact he is initially reluctant. It was God Himself who motivated and commissioned Moses. It has been well said by many that, 'When God calls, He equips. When God calls, He enables'. Also note that while the *'Angel of the LORD'* was involved in motivating Moses, the proclaiming of God's message to the people was to be completed by Moses. This Biblical feature is a continuing responsibility for God's people today – Mark 16:15; Romans 10:14.

Balaam – Blindness that was Banished 'There's nowt so queer as folk' is an expression mostly used in the North of England to emphasize that some people behave in very strange ways. Such a phrase could well be applied to Balaam; he had some very bizarre ways. He was a deceitful character who was easily seduced by worldly appeasements. He was a greedy man who was out to make money through his religious activities (Jude 1:11). You can read the full account of his antics in the book of Numbers chapters 22-25. The Lord Jesus Christ had cause to warn a church about the *'the doctrine of Balaam'* (Rev. 2:14).

The hymn writer, William Cowper (1731-1800) reminds us that, 'God moves in a mysterious way His wonders to perform'. God did a mysterious thing when He permitted Balaam's donkey to see *'the Angel of the LORD'.* This was even before Balaam's eyes were opened to see Him. This is also one of those mysterious and rare occasions when God used an animal to accomplish His purposes. Compare Jonah 1:17 and Matthew 17:27.

Joshua – Directives about Demolition During the 1990s there were many archaeological excavations in Palestine. Unfortunately the motive for many of these seems to have been a desire to disprove the accuracy of the Bible. Some archaeologist reported that they had found evidence the walls of Jericho did **not** fall down as recorded in Joshua chapter 6. It was only after subsequent excavations were completed that the flattened walls of the city were discovered. The latest archaeological evidence agrees with the summarised statement of Hebrews 11:30.

Joshua was the leader of the nation of Israel at the time of the battle. His predecessor, Moses, together with the people of Israel, was assured by God that *'My Angel will go before you …'* (Exod. 23:23). Note that once again, the title *'the Angel of the LORD'* does not occur in this passage. However, the characteristics of the *'Man'* and the fact that He was *'worshipped'* by Joshua indicate that He is divine. Note the use of the capital letter; this was no mere mortal but His appearance was that of a man. Many writers, like me, are convinced that this is the *'the Angel of the LORD',* the pre-incarnate Son of God.

Manoah – A Son named Samson If you began a conversation about the son of William and his wife Morrow, I can imagine many will be asking, 'Who are they?' They were the parents of the internationally famous preacher Dr Billy Graham. We know who their son is even though we are unaware of his parents' names. It is highly probable that you know of Samson. A person with unusually great strength is said to have the 'strength of Samson'. Manoah and his unnamed wife were Samson's parents. This remarkable man served the Lord and the nation of Israel. This was during the period in their history when *'the LORD raised up judges who delivered them'* (Judg. 2:16). Samson was very different from the other judges whom God raised up to deliver Israel from an oppressive enemy.

Samson, like Jeremiah (Jer. 1:5) and John the Baptist (Luke 1:11-17), was not chosen when he had become an established leader, he was chosen by God prior to birth. Samson's parents were informed about their additional family member and their son's dedicated life style by *'the Angel of the LORD'.*

Elijah – Commissioned and Consoled Having been threatened by Queen Jezebel (1 Kings 19:2) Elijah fled for his life. Now the voice of *'the Angel of the LORD'* is heard by God's prophet. He is sometimes respectfully addressed as the *'Man of God',* possibly due to the divine interventions associated with his ministry. Notice he refers to himself humbly as, *'a man of God'* (v. 10). Elijah is now coming to the end of his public service; his mantle will soon fall on his successor Elisha. Elijah is first informed who he is to meet, what he is to say. Subsequently the heavenly messenger directs and reassures him.

Supplementary Notes to Study 7

– The 'angel of the Lord' New Testament references

There are twelve references in the New Testament (NT) to *'the'* or *'an angel of the Lord'.* These are holy angels whom God has created. This description must not be confused with the Old Testament (OT) title *'the Angel of the LORD'.* This title is given to the pre-incarnation of Jesus Christ, the eternal Son of God, who appeared during the OT period. In the NT, that is, since the incarnation of the Lord Jesus Christ, He is never referred to as *'the Angel of the LORD'.* There is just one exception in the NT, namely Acts 7:30. In this case the author of Acts is writing about Moses' encounter with the divine person in the OT.

Note from the references listed below that the most common NT phrase referring to angels is, *'an angel of the Lord'.* This indicates that the angel is one of many. The translators and printers of our English Bible rightly use the lower case letter 'a' repeatedly in the word *'angel',* indicating that this is a created being.

Matthew 1:24 is the only occasion in the NT when the definite article is used – *'the angel of the Lord'.* It is referring back to *'an angel of the Lord'* (Matt. 1:20).

Matt. 1:20 *'But while he thought about these things, behold, an* ***angel of the Lord*** *appeared to him in a dream …'*

Matt. 1:24 *'Then Joseph, being aroused from sleep, did as the* ***angel of the Lord*** *commanded him …'*

Matt. 2:13 *'… an* ***angel of the Lord*** *appeared to Joseph in a dream …'*

Matt. 2:19 *'Now when Herod was dead, behold, an* ***angel of the Lord*** *appeared in a dream to Joseph in Egypt …'*

Matt. 28:2 *'And behold, there was a great earthquake; for an* ***angel of the Lord*** *descended from heaven …'*

Luke 1:11 *'Then an* ***angel of the Lord*** *appeared to him …'*

Luke 2:9 *'And behold, an* ***angel of the Lord*** *stood before them …'*

Acts 5:19 *But at night an* ***angel of the Lord*** *opened the prison doors …'*

Acts 7:30 *'And when forty years had passed, an* ***Angel of the Lord*** *appeared to him in a flame of fire in a bush …'*

Acts 8:26 *'Now an* ***angel of the Lord*** *spoke to Philip, saying …'*

Acts 12:7 *'Now behold, an* ***angel of the Lord*** *stood by him, and a light shone in the prison …'*

Acts 12:23 *'Then immediately an* ***angel of the Lord*** *struck him …'*

STUDY 8

THE SAVIOUR'S ASSOCIATION WITH ANGELS

QUESTIONS

Day 1 Christ's Incarnation – His miraculous birth
Matthew 1:18-21; Luke 1:5-20 & 26-38; Luke 2:8-15.

a) What are we told about the angel who appeared to Zachariah and Mary?

b) Who was the angel's message to the shepherds focused upon?

c) The fact that the same message was given to Joseph (Matt. 1:20); Zacharias (Luke 1:13); Mary (Luke 1:30) and the shepherds (Luke 2:10) – what does this indicate about the ministry of angels?

Day 2 Christ's Temptation – His personal conflict with the Devil
Matthew 4:1-11; Mark 1: 13; Hebrews 4:14-16.

a) Why was the ministry of angels required by the Saviour at this time?

b) Believers may not always have the ministry of angels to sympathise and help, but how can we get help, especially in times of temptation?

Day 3 Christ's Tuition – His enlightening ministry
Luke 20:34-39; Matthew 13:36-44; Matthew 26:47-56.

a) As Jesus answers a question about marriage and the resurrection what did He indirectly teach about angels?

b) In Christ's *'kingdom of heaven'* parables what is the role of the angels?

c) How can the statement of Jesus about angels, at the time of his arrest in Gethsemane, be of consolation to us?

Day 4 Christ's Crucifixion – His atoning death
Matthew 16:21-23; Luke 22:39-44; 1 Peter 1:10-12.

a) Why did the Lord Jesus Christ say to Peter, *'Get behind me, Satan!'*?

QUESTIONS (contd)

b) Who came from heaven to strengthen Christ as he faced death by crucifixion?

c) What is it that the *'angels desire to look into'*?

Day 5 Christ's Resurrection – His triumph over death

Matthew 28:1-8; Luke 24:1-12.

a) What impact did the encounter with the angel have on the guards and the two Marys?

b) Despite the angel's triumphant message, what was the initial reaction of the eleven disciples to the news of Christ's resurrection?

Day 6 Christ's Ascension – His visible return to heaven

Acts 1:9-11; 1 Peter 3:18-22.

a) What message of reassurance did the angels have for the disciples at the time of Christ's ascension?

b) Where is Christ now and what is the position of the angels in relationship to Him?

Day 7 Christ's Jubilation – His promised return to earth

Matthew 25:31; Mark 8:38; 1 Thessalonians 4:16-18.

a) Who will accompany Christ when He returns in His glory as promised?

b) Do you have any reason to be ashamed of Jesus?

c) How are the Apostle Paul's words a comfort to Christians?

NOTES

Do you remember the torturous childhood experience of waiting for Christmas day to arrive when you could get to open your presents at last! The special number 25 seemed to take forever to get to on the Advent Calendar. Imagine what it must have been like for God's people waiting to hear the angels bring *'good tidings of great joy'* about the promised Saviour. The Old Testament scriptures end with God's message via the prophet Malachi. For four long centuries there had been only silence. Then as the New Testament era dawns, Matthew records the good news of Christ's coming. Both Matthew and Luke inform us about a flurry of angelic activity. From this flow other details of how angels were involved in the Saviour's ministry and the inclusion of angels in His teaching. Note carefully how the New Testament angel's activities centre upon the person of Jesus Christ. The angels do not seek praise or draw attention to themselves. Their aim is to draw attention to their Creator and the Redeemer of sinners. Although Christ was, *'made a little lower than the angels, for the suffering of death'* He was then *'crowned with glory and honour'* (Ps. 8:5; Heb. 2:7 & 9). We need to keep in mind that Christ is *'so much better than the angels'* (Heb. 1:4). This is why they are told, *'Let all the angels of God worship Him'* (Heb. 1:6). This week's study is a brief survey of Christ's association with angels. These incidents start with Christ's first coming and conclude with His promised return.

Christ's Incarnation – His miraculous birth The heavenly messengers came with a series of truly amazing announcements. An elderly couple, Zacharias and Elizabeth are told that they are going to have a son named John. A virgin young lady is informed that she also is going to deliver a baby boy to be named Jesus, but in her case the conception was the miraculous work of the Holy Spirit. Poor Joseph, Mary's future husband, is astonished and needs to be reassured. Also, a normally socially isolated group of people, some shepherds, get to hear about the *'Saviour who is Christ the Lord'.* Then they get to hear a choir formed of *'a multitude of the heavenly host'.*

Christ's Temptation – His personal conflict with the Devil Christ, the Creator of *'all things'* (Col. 1:16), who was *'made a little lower than the angels'* (Heb. 2:7) endured a threefold attack by the leading fallen angel, Satan. Having suffered for forty days in the wilderness, in solitude amongst wild beasts, Christ vanquished Satan and was then ministered to by angels. This would eventually lead up to the Saviour becoming the sympathising and sinless High Priest of all who believe in Him.

Christ's Tuition – His enlightening ministry In a letter he once wrote, the English non-conformist minister Philip Doddridge (1702-1751) described a man as having a 'bee in his bonnet'. I have had cause to use the expression when a fellow preacher appeared to be preoccupied with one particular topic. This topic study of angels may lead some to think that I am rather obsessed with this biblical topic. However, this could never be said of the balanced ministry of the world's greatest preacher and teacher, the Lord Jesus Christ. The Saviour referred to angels frequently and unashamedly. He always did so in an appropriate and often in illustrative ways. Christ's ministry indicates that He was mindful of their existence, nature and useful functions. Out of the four Gospel writers it is Matthew who records the most of Christ's references to angels. This limited survey of the Lord's enlightening ministry serves as a reminder that angels are 'not just for Christmas'!

Christ's Crucifixion – His atoning death The song writer, telling of Christ's purpose for leaving the ecstasy of heaven to come to the misery of earth has said,

'Yet You left the gaze of angels,
came to seek and save the lost,
and exchanged the joy of heaven
for the anguish of the cross.' [1]

Christ's crucifixion would have been the last thing that the fallen angel Satan would have wanted. He was aware of the ancient prophecy that Christ would bruise Satan's head (Gen. 3:15) at Calvary. Jesus was aware that in order to gain the victor's crown, He had to voluntarily suffer on the cross (John 10:18). For a moment even Peter, one of the Lord's close apostles, failed to understand the necessity of Christ's atoning death. Satan had briefly managed to influence Peter's thinking and he was promptly corrected by the Lord. An angel of the Lord had clearly instructed at the time of Christ's incarnation, *'you shall call His name Jesus, for He shall save His people from their sins'* (Matt. 1:21). While He came *'to give His life a ransom for many on the cross'* (Matt. 20:28) Christ's death did not redeem even one fallen angel. The holy angels enjoy God's presence and do not need to be pardoned. The fallen angels are banished from God's presence and will never be granted a pardon. God's *'elect angels'* can only watch the Lord working out His plan of salvation with amazement and a holy curiosity.

Christ's Resurrection – His triumph over death During His earthly ministry Jesus spoke of *'a certain beggar named Lazarus'.* The Lord said that he *'was carried by angels'* to heaven when he died (Luke 16:22). Following the death of the Saviour on the cross it is reported that *'an angel of the Lord descended from heaven ... and rolled back the stone'* from the Lord's grave (Matt. 28:2). These details indicate that there is often angelic activity around the time of a godly person's death. In the case of Christ, the angel removed the huge stone from the grave, not so much as to let Jesus out but to let the disciple look into the empty grave. Yet again the heavenly messengers appeared in the form of men. Their dazzling appearance terrified some, while their message reassured others.

Christ's Ascension – His visible return to heaven Even when you know that someone whom you love dearly is leaving to go to heaven, the parting can be very tough. The faithful disciples were going to miss the physical presence of their beloved Lord and Master. God is gracious in supporting those who love Him at such times. Just as angels were sent in human appearance with words of reassurance following the Saviour's death (Luke 24:4) so now two are sent on the day of the Lord's ascension. The Saviour had said to His followers *'if I go and prepare a place for you, I will come again and receive you to Myself'* (John 14:3). The angels' question to the disciples on Ascension Day was not said to rebuke but to remind and reassure them. Later the Apostle Paul wrote saying of Christ that He was *'Seen by angels ... Received up in glory'* (I Tim. 3:16).

Christ's Jubilation – His promised return to earth Depending upon our personal relationship with Christ the day of the Lord's return will either be a day of dread or a day of delight. The grand old hymn of Charles Wesley (1707-1788) puts it so well:

1. Stuart Townend and Keith Getty © 2002 Thankyou Music.

Thou judge of quick and dead,
Before whose bar severe,
With holy joy, or guilty dread,
We all shall soon appear.

Our cautioned souls prepare
For that tremendous day,
And fill us now with watchful care,
And stir us up to pray.

To pray, and wait the hour,
That wondrous hour unknown,
When, robed in majesty and power,
Thou shalt from Heaven come down.

The immortal Son of Man,
To judge the human race,
With all Thy Father's dazzling train,
With all Thy glorious grace.

O may we thus be found
Obedient to His Word
Attentive to the trumpet's sound,
And looking for our Lord!

STUDY 9

AMAZING ACCOMPLISHMENTS

QUESTIONS

Day 1 **Suffering but not Silenced** *Acts 5:17-32; John 16:33; 2 Timothy 3:12.*

a) What were Peter and the apostles able to do as a result of the *'angel of the Lord'* opening the prison doors?

b) How did the Saviour both advise and assure His followers about suffering in the world?

c) What is the difficulty that those living a godly life are warned of by the Apostle Paul?

Day 2 **Believers' Baptism** *Matthew 28:18-20; Acts 1:8-9; Acts 8:26-40.*

a) Who did Jesus say were to be baptised?

b) What was Christ's final declaration and obligation to His disciples, before ascending to heaven?

c) Having been directed by an angel, how was Philip able to assist the Ethiopian eunuch?

Day 3 **Good news for the Gentiles** *Acts 10:1-43 & 11:13-14.*

a) What do we learn from the experience that Cornelius had with the angel who conversed with him? (See Acts 10:3, 7, 30 & 11:13).

b) What was the serious mistake Cornelius made on meeting Peter?

Day 4 **Punished for Preaching** *Acts12:1-19; 1 Peter 4:12-16.*

a) Why was Peter in prison?

b) What made Peter's deliverance from prison by the *'angel of the Lord'* such a timely one?

QUESTIONS (contd)

c) When should Christians be willing to suffer?

Day 5 **Wriggly Worms!** *Acts12:20-25; Proverbs 16:18.*

a) What stands out the most to you about the affliction imposed by the angel of the Lord?

b) What was the positive outcome from the angel afflicting Herod?

c) What does pride go before?

Day 6 **Dissension and Deliverance** *Acts 23:1-10.*

a) What did the Pharisees and Sadducees disagree over?

b) Why do you think these matters are important?

Day 7 **Shipwrecked but Saved** *Acts 27:13-44; Psalm 34:7.*

a) What were the circumstances of the Apostle Paul when the angel stood by him?

b) Why was the angel's message so helpful for the Apostle and all aboard the ship?

NOTES

The Bible book we know as 'The Acts of the Apostles' is an exciting account of first century church history.

It contains clear evidence of Christ's prediction being fulfilled – *'I will build My church, and the gates of Hades shall not prevail against it'* (Matt. 16:18). It was both a period of triumph for the gospel and tribulation for the godly. Mingled amongst the 'acts of the apostles' are the 'amazing accomplishments of angels'. In this study we shall consider the circumstances and significance of the angel's accomplishments that supported the spread of the gospel of God's grace.

Suffering but not Silenced Have you ever had cause to admire the remarkable strength of a person who has endured great suffering or difficulty without complaining? We often admire such a person for their ability to 'Suffer in Silence'. However, there will be times when Satan will try and silence Christians in direct opposition to the Lord's command to speak. The Lord Jesus Christ warned His disciples about this and assured them that the Holy Spirit would teach them what to say in such times (Luke 12:11-12). Christ said to the members of a local church, *'Do not fear any of those things which you are about to suffer. Indeed, the devil is about to throw some of you into prison …'* (Rev. 2:10). What an example the apostles and the first century Christians have shown us by their willingness to suffer, but not be silent (Acts 4:18-20)!

Believers' Baptism Christians should expect the unexpected, especially when they seek to faithfully serve the Lord. Philip was experiencing what sounds like a God-sent revival in the city of Samaria (Acts 8:4-8). Multitudes of people were hearing the gospel. Then unexpectedly, *'an angel of the Lord'* instructs Philip to leave town on a dusty desert road to help an individual understand the Gospel, an Ethiopian. The universal nature of Christ's gospel is now seen bursting from its Jewish beginnings; it is rippling out from Jerusalem to the Gentiles. It pleased the Lord to help an African man understand the Scriptures by having an angel direct Philip to him. Surely this high ranking official must have been amongst the first of many Africans to have been baptised as a Believer.

Good news for the Gentiles The Apostle John warns us, *'do not believe every spirit, but test the spirits, whether they are of God; because many false prophets have gone out into the world'* (1 John 4:1). I have read some strange claims made by people having visions and seeing angels that have given me concern. When such reports do not remotely resemble the accounts about angels in the Bible I am rather sceptical. However, we know the Bible accounts are God inspired (2 Tim. 3:16) and therefore reliable. In the middle of the afternoon the Roman Centurion, Cornelius, saw an *'angel of God'* in a vision. The angel's directive was the means of helping and enlightening Cornelius, his household, the Apostle Peter and the Jewish church leaders. It stimulated evangelism among the Gentiles (people who are not Jews) and also the acceptance of Gentile converts into the church.

Punished for Preaching If you have a 'déjà vu' feeling about the record in Acts 12 concerning Peter's deliverance from prison, it is understandable. On day one of this week's study, we considered how an angel of the Lord opened the prison doors for the gospel preachers enabling them to get on with their work. We must not presume that because God used an angel to bring about an early release of the Apostles from prison sometimes, that He will do so every time. This may not always be in the will of God. Paul stated that his imprisonment *'turned out for the furtherance of the gospel'* (Phil. 1:12). Peter's further deliverance from prison certainly astonished the people in the prayer meeting that night. Ironically, he had more trouble getting into Mary's house where the prayer meeting was taking place than he had getting out of a top security prison! Note that when the task was completed then, *'immediately the angel departed'.* Angels appear to be rather shy creatures and they certainly do not hang around in the hope of being praised for what they have done.

Wriggly Worms! There was a dark and cruel streak in Herod's character that increasingly showed itself. Having dared to murder James, one of the Lord's closest disciples, he would have gladly eliminated the Apostle Peter also. The first century Jewish historian, Josephus, wrote about the occasion of Herod's speech that invoked God's anger and judgement. '... early in the morning of the celebration, the king arrayed himself in a garment woven with silver threads. When the sun's rays fell upon that robe it glittered and shone with a resplendence that dazzled the crowds packed into the theatre.' However, his time for basking in his own glory soon came to an abrupt end! Such is the Lord's mercy that immediate judgements of this nature are rare, but they do happen sometimes. Well might the Apostle Paul remind us, *'Do not be deceived, God is not mocked; for whatever a man sows, that he will also reap. For he who sows to his flesh will of the flesh reap corruption ...'* (Gal. 6:7-8).

Dissension and Deliverance The Pharisees were a legalistic and religious 'separatist' group of Jews. They claimed to resolutely keep themselves away from any type of impurity prescribed by the Levitical law. Sadly, their religion was often only outward show, with little sincerity of heart. They developed an increasing resentment to Christ and the early Christians. Prior to his conversion the Apostle Paul was a strict Pharisee (Phil. 3:5).

The Pharisaic *'sect of the Sadducees'* (Acts 5:17) were also early opponents of Jesus and the early Christians (Acts 4:1-3). They are frequently found conveniently forgetting their doctrinal differences, so as to be joining forces with the Pharisees in opposition to Christ and His followers. The two significant things that the Sadducees did not believe were the reality of the resurrection and the existence of angels. Paul took advantage of the theological disagreement between the Sadducees and the Pharisees and caused a major disruption in the Jewish Council.

Shipwrecked but Saved We live in an age when satellite navigation is common place. Space rockets, aeroplanes, ships and cars all have a guidance system that has pinpoint accuracy. Many of our mobile phones have a map that discloses precise location so that we can be located in an emergency. No such technology was available to Julius the Roman centurion in the first century. When he was escorting the Apostle Paul and other prisoners by sea, there was no means of sending an SOS message when a severe storm arose. Paul, along with everyone else on the ship were helpless and in danger of drowning. Neither they nor anyone else knew their location, but the angel of God did. God required Paul to appear before Caesar who needed to hear the gospel before he died. God's special agent, an angel, was dispatched to reassure God's Apostle who was about to be shipwrecked, but saved.

STUDY 10

THE ANGELS' FINAL AWESOME ACTIVITIES

QUESTIONS

Day 1 **Humble Adoration** *Revelation 5:7-14 & 7:9-12; Psalm 96:1-4.*

a) What is the main activity of the angels and the other occupants of heaven?

b) Who is being worshipped and adored?

c) Why might this song be called a 'Missionary Song'?

Day 2 **Thought-provoking Question** *Revelation 5:1-7 & 17:1-7.*

a) Having heard the angel's first question what was John's reaction and how was he reassured?

b) The angel asked John, *'Why did you marvel?'* What is your reaction to what was disclosed about the *'Mother of Harlots?'*

Day 3 **Universal Proclamation** *Revelation 14:1-13; Ezekiel 33:11.*

a) What was the theme of the message said with a *'loud voice'*, by the first of the three angels?

b) Why would God want such a message to be heard by all on earth?

Day 4 **Merciful Preservation** *Revelation 7:1-8; Psalm 125:1-2; John 10:27-30.*

a) Why were *'four angels'* required to be involved in the work of preservation?

b) In addition to the ministry of angels, what reassurance is given by the Psalmist and Christ of the safeguarding of God's people?

QUESTIONS (contd)

Day 5 **Just Condemnation**
Revelation 15:7 – 16:2; Matthew 25:41-46; Romans 8:1.

a) Who are involved in pouring out God's wrath and who are being condemned?

b) What assurance do you have of not having to face God's just condemnation?

Day 6 **Ardent Jubilation** *Revelation 19:1-10; 1 Thessalonians 5:16-18.*

a) What two events, one of condemnation and one of celebration, caused jubilation in heaven?

b) When do you find it most difficult to comply with the Apostle Paul's exhortation?

Day 7 **Earnest Expectation** *Revelation 22:6-21; John 14:1-3; Acts 1:11.*

a) What was inappropriate about the Apostle John's reaction before the angel?

b) In an age when many are saying of Christ, *'Where is the promise of His coming?'* (2 Pet. 3:4), what is it that gives Christians an earnest expectation that it will happen?

NOTES

So often we abbreviate the name of the last book of the Bible to 'Revelation', but we should not forget that it is, 'The Revelation of Jesus Christ'. He made it known by sending His angel to the Apostle John. As we have seen in a previous study the Lord Jesus Christ is closely associated with the *'holy angels'.* He predicted that He would return, *'in the glory of His Father with the holy angels'.* In this short survey of some of the angels' final activities we shall be thinking about the angels who are heavenly spirits. Hence it will not include the angels, the human servants (messengers) of the seven churches (Rev. chapters 2–3). This amazing vision of future events demonstrates that God's angels have a dual ministry. At the Lord's command they defend and destroy, they preserve and punish. They also rejoice over all that God will accomplish for His glory and the good of His people.

Humble Adoration I once had the privilege of hearing the 'London Emmanuel Choir', an all Christian group of chorister, singing in the Royal Albert Hall. Listening to their songs of praise reverberating around the venue was a thrilling experience. If that experience was so memorable what must it be like in heaven, with a vast number of heavenly host all praising the Lord? Our Bible translation of *'many angels'* is a gross understatement for a choir of countless angels. The implication is that there were several millions of them. They had twin themes of praise, for God's creation and God's redemption.

In the vision Christ is represented as the *'Lamb who was slain'* (compare John 1:29). The *'new song'* is being sung in recognition of the new covenant Christ has established by the shedding of His blood (Matt. 26:28; Heb. 8:13).

Thought-provoking Question If you have ever had to care for young children you may, at times, have been tempted to ask them, 'Why do you ask so many questions?' Apparently, there are at least fifteen different reasons why questions are asked. Twice in the Book of Revelation it is stated that an angel asked a question. The first question relates to a symbolic sealed scroll, the second to a figurative wicked woman. The reason for an angel asking a question is different in each case.

The first question was asked to provoke a thoughtful anticipation of the forthcoming answer. The answer to the question focused on the Lord Jesus Christ. He is the one who is both worthy to reveal God's plan and who has the power to carry it out.

The angel asked the Apostle John the second question in view of the horrifying things shown to him. John appears confused and astonished. He was expected to have anticipated the corrupting influence of evil.

Universal Proclamation Beware of an inappropriate deduction from the statement in Revelation 14:6 about the angel *'flying'.* Other than creatures such as a cherubim and seraphim, angels do not have wings, even though artists usually give them a pair. Earthly creatures, like birds and butterflies, require wings to fly due to the law of aerodynamics. Angels are spirits who can travel backwards and forwards from and to heaven without the need of wings. Also, keep in mind that this is an account of a vision. Some very strange things are seen and heard in visions that are not experienced in real-life on earth. For example an enraged dragon may occur in a vision (Rev. 12:7), but they do not exist as real creatures on earth. Neither do angels have the responsibility of preaching *'the everlasting gospel on earth – to every nation, tribe, tongue and people'.* God's people have been charged with that responsibility (Matt. 28:16-20; Mark 16:14-16).

Merciful Preservation The hymn writer, Augustus Toplady (1740-78) wrote, 'A sovereign Protector I have, unseen, yet ever at hand, unchangeably faithful to save'. One of the main tasks of God's angels seen throughout the Scriptures is to protect God's people. The *'four angels'* (Rev. 7:1) are charged with a protective role by the *'angel ascending from the east'.* This permitted the angel to put a seal on *'the servants of our God'.* The seal denotes ownership, they belong to the Lord (Eph. 1:13). This merciful preservation does **not** mean that Christians, the *'Israel of God'* (Gal. 6:16) will not *'suffer for righteousness sake'* (1 Pet. 3:14). However, on the final judgement day they will be preserved *'from the wrath of the Lamb!'* (Rev. 6:16). On that day, *'God will wipe away every tear from their eyes'* (Rev. 7:17).

Just Condemnation It has often been said that there are more references in Scripture to the anger, fury, and wrath of God, than there are to His love and tenderness. This may be an indication that there is so much sin and evil in this fallen world that provokes the Almighty. It is also a reminder that God has such a strong abhorrence for sin and injustice. The Apostle Paul reminds us that we must *'all appear before the judgment seat of Christ'* (Rom. 14:10; 2 Cor. 5:10). Even the angels are not exempt from God's perfect justice and condemnation (Jude 1:6). Revelation chapter 15 is an introduction to *'seven angels'* who are charged to *'go and pour out the bowls of the wrath of God on the earth'* (Rev. 16:1). This is followed by several chapters of symbols that portray God's wrath. God's holy angels are involved in condemning evil and will observe the Lord's just indignation of unrighteousness (Rev. 14:10).

Ardent Jubilation George Frideric Handel composed his now famous oratorio the 'Messiah' in 1741. If you have never heard it before please make a point of listening to the section known as the 'Hallelujah Chorus'. It is quite phenomenal when sung by a talented choir. It will give you a little foretaste of something even more spectacular recorded in Revelation chapter 19. The jubilant praise had an overwhelming impact upon the Apostle John when it was revealed to him by the Lord's angel (Rev. 1:1). In his indescribable joy, John fell at the feet of God's special messenger *'to worship him'* (Rev. 19:10) and was promptly reprimanded. The Hebrew word, 'Hallelujah' means 'Praise the Lord'. It is used here as an authoritative command and an expression of joyful praise. The great multitude in heaven are not rejoicing in the eternal damnation of the wicked, but rather that justice has been done, and the fact that the *'Lord God Omnipotent reigns!'* (Rev. 19:6).

Earnest Expectation The voice of Christ's martyrs was previously heard crying out *'with a loud voice, saying, "How long, O Lord, holy and true, until You judge and avenge our blood on those who dwell on the earth?"'* (Rev. 6:10). While we do not know *'the day nor the hour in which the Son of Man is coming'* (Matt. 25:13), we can be confident that God always keeps His promises. The last chapter of the Bible records the Saviour's words, *'I, Jesus, have sent My angel to testify to you these things ...' 'Surely I am coming quickly'* (Rev. 22:16 & 20). Every Christian should be thankful for what the Lord's angel has disclosed in this last book of the Bible. We should be even more grateful that God has granted access to the eternal city, heaven, and that our names are in the *'Lamb's Book of Life'* (Rev. 21:27). There is an *'earnest expectation'* on the part of creation (Rom. 8:19-22) and every Believer for the day when, *'the Son of Man comes in His glory, and all the holy angels with Him ...'* (Matt. 25:31).

STUDY 11

THE ASSISTANCE OF ANGELS

QUESTIONS

Day 1 **Protecting** *Psalm 91:9-16.*

a) Share the details with the group if you have personally experienced, or if you have heard of someone who sensed God's protection as mentioned in verse 11?

b) What impresses you about John F. Paton's experience of being protected? (See this week's notes – Protecting)

c) What is your reaction to the six *'I will'* statements in the Psalm (vv. 14-16)?

Day 2 **Defending** *Psalm 34:7; Daniel 6:21-23.*

a) What group of people should be encouraged by the Psalmist's statement?

b) How did God ensure that His servant Daniel was delivered from danger?

c) What does Donavan's (See this week's notes - Defending) and Daniel's experience have in common?

Day 3 **Encouraging** *Psalm 3:1-4; Psalm 119:145-148, Amos 8:11.*

a) What were the key features in the experience of the Psalmist and Corrie ten Boom (See this week's notes – Encouraging) that encouraged them in their time of difficulty?

b) Why would not having a Bible available to read be of concern to many?

QUESTIONS (contd)

Day 4 **Guiding** *Genesis 19:15-17; Psalm 32:8-9.*

a) Whom did God use to guide Lot and his family to safety?

b) Why was the guidance given to Lot and Marlene (See this week's notes - Guiding) so critical?

c) What are the positive and negative elements of the Psalmist's comments about guidance?

Day 5 **Helping** *Psalm 121:1-8; 2 Kings 6:8-18; Numbers 22:31.*

a) What is your response to the assurance of help spoken of by the Psalmist?

b) What is the evidence that it is possible to be helped by angels and yet not always see them?

Day 6 **Reassuring** *Acts 27:13-26; Hebrews 1:5-14.*

a) How was the Apostle Paul reassured on his hazardous journey?

b) Who are the *'ministering spirits'* spoken of in Hebrews and referred to by John Paton (See this week's notes – Reassuring) and how did they reassure him?

Day 7 **Comforting** *Luke 16:19-23; John 14:1-3; Psalm 116:15.*

a) What are the main contrasting features between the death of *'Lazarus'* and the *'rich man'*?

b) What is a great source of comfort to Christians as they face death?

NOTES

When we read or hear accounts of angelic interventions we need to be cautious. Why? Because 'Fake News' abounds about angels! There are sensational fictitious as well as factual accounts of angels. The Apostle Paul reminds us that Satan, a fallen angel, is the world's best deceiver. *'... Satan himself transforms himself into an angel of light'* (2 Cor. 11:14). Dr Billy Graham, commenting on an amazing deliverance that has been attributed to angels said, 'During my ministry I have heard or read literally thousands of similar stories. Could it be that these were hallucinations or accidents or fate or luck? Or were real angels sent from God to perform certain tasks?'[1] We need to test the stories we hear and compare them with the accounts that are recorded in the Scriptures and see how they compare. The Biblical principle for testing error or accuracy is, *'by the mouth of two or three witnesses the matter shall be established'* [Deut. 19:15].

For each of the following illustrative accounts on the continuing ministry of angels in this week's studies I have done my best to ensure that they are authentic. We would do well to follow the Apostle Paul's instruction, *'Test all things; hold fast what is good'* (1 Thess. 5:21).

Protecting: Reverend John G. Paton (1824-1907), pioneer missionary in the New Hebrides Islands, told a thrilling story involving the protective care of angels. Hostile natives surrounded his mission headquarters one night, intent on burning the Patons' house and killing them. John Paton and his wife prayed during all that terror-filled night that God would deliver them. When daylight came they were amazed to see that, unaccountably, the attackers had left. They thanked God for delivering them.

A year later, the chief of the tribe was converted to Jesus Christ, and Mr Paton, remembering what had happened, asked the chief what had kept him and his men from burning down the house and killing them. The chief replied in surprise, 'Who were all those men you had with you there?' The missionary answered, 'There were no men there; just my wife and I.' The chief argued that they had seen many men standing guard – hundreds of big men in shining garments with drawn swords in their hands. They seemed to circle the mission station so that the natives were afraid to attack. Only then did Mr Paton realize that God had sent His angels to protect them. The chief agreed that there was no other explanation. Could it be that God had sent a legion of angels to protect His servants, whose lives were being endangered?[2]

Defending: Donavan Cox is described by the author, Hope Price, who met him as, '... sane and sensible... not a man given to visions or fancy, and this was the only extraordinary experience that he has ever had'. During the Second World War, in the autumn of 1941, London was blitzed for sixty consecutive nights. Donavan and his wife Doris lived in Ealing, West London. They had made a downstairs room as safe as possible and slept there at night.

1. **Angels – God's Secret Agents**, Billy Graham, Hodder and Stoughton, London, 1975, Revised Edition 1986 (p. 17-18) ISBN 0-340-63031-0.

2. Cited in **Angels – God's Secret Agents**, Billy Graham, Hodder and Stoughton, London, Revised Edition 1986 (pp. 16-17) ISBN 0-340-63031-0.

One evening, at about 9 p.m., Donavan said to his wife, 'There's going to be a disturbance tonight, but we will be kept safe, so there is no need to worry.' Doris asked; 'How do you know?' Donavan explained; 'I can see an angel above our house protecting us.' He saw a huge figure in the form of a person with outstretched arms floating about twenty feet above the house. Donavan says, 'I knew for certain that the angel was there, and I knew something would happen that night.' About 2 a.m. there was a loud explosion above the house that woke them. The doors were burst open by the tremendous blast. However, to their amazement nothing else was damaged. They were able to go back to sleep and then about 8 a.m. the street warden, on the lookout for bomb damage called on them. He explained that there had been a parachute bomb that had come down over their house and exploded in mid-air. Such a bomb was designed to detonate on impact with an object. It should not have exploded harmlessly in the air. There were two other independent witnesses that night, who knew nothing of the angelic appearance, who confirmed the location of the descending bomb. Hope Price reports that, 'Donavan was totally convinced about the angel he had seen ... He appreciated just how great God's protection had been.' [3]

Encouraging: Corrie ten Boom (1892-1983) endured ten months in the horrific German concentration camp in Ravensbrück. Her crime was hiding Jews in her family's home in Holland. Everything was confiscated from the prisoners. In an interview Corrie ten Boom testified that it was a 'miracle' that she was able to get a Bible into the camp. 'When we entered, I had a little Bible, a small Bible but a whole Bible, Old and New Testament, and I had it hidden under my clothing on my back. I saw that they took away everything what we had hidden, and I was so scared that I said, 'O Lord, send Your angels, that they surround me.' But then I thought, Yes, but angels are spirits and you can look through a spirit and these people may not see me, *so* I said, 'O God, let Your angels this time not be transparent.' God did it. The woman who stood before me was searched and then my sister who was behind me. They did not see me, so I came in the prison with my Bible.' [4]

What an incredible source of encouragement this was to Corrie to see her prayer answered! What a marvellous encouragement it was to many of the prisoners, having a Bible available in their appalling circumstances.

Guiding: Marlene Wiechman, of West Point, Nebraska, USA believes angels helped her when her daughter, Emily, was six years old. Emily had had a stroke at seven months and was left partially handicapped. While they were on a family holiday Emily became very ill. Marlene states that, 'We went on vacation with my parents to Yellowstone National Park. On the way home, driving through Wyoming, Emily said she didn't feel well. She started vomiting and her eyes weren't focusing. We needed to get her to a hospital, but the nearest town, Rock Springs, was 70 miles away. Emily kept getting worse, and as we approached Rock Springs, I prayed we would find help quickly. Just then, we saw a blue and white hospital sign. There were three or four more signs that led us straight to the emergency room.'

A doctor at the hospital was able to give the prompt attention required. When Marlene spoke of the road signs being a lifesaver, the doctor exclaimed, 'What signs?' He explained that he

3. **Angels – True stories of how they touch our lives**, Hope Price, Macmillan, London, 1993 – Pan Books edition 1994 (pp. 8-9) ISBN 0-330-32850-6.

4. **INTERVIEW by Pat Robinson of the Christian Broadcasting Network [CBN] 700 Club** http://www1.cbn.com/700club/faith-not-hidden

travelled on that road every day, and there were no such signs. All four adults travelling in the vehicle had seen them. They returned to look once more but they were gone! Further enquiries were made and they were told that there never had been any hospital signs on that route. Marlene concluded, 'I believe they were put there for us by God or His angels.'[5]

Helping: David Rushworth-Smith (1927-2011), who in his early days as a Baptist pastor was not able to afford a car, was riding a motorcycle. He set off about 9.30 p.m. one snowy night in the winter of 1953, after speaking in a little church at Kersey in Suffolk. The conditions were dangerous as it had snowed heavily and was now freezing. As David was proceeding carefully along, the road seemed to suddenly slide from under him and he shot across to the right hand side, straight towards a pile of hard ice. He says, 'I was all alone, miles from anywhere and knew that if I hit the ice and was hurt I could freeze to death. In a split second I prayed for help and I saw a strong pair of hands [took] hold of the handlebars. They picked up the bike, with me still on it, while it slid across the road, almost on its side. The hands put the motorcycle and myself back on the crown of the road, still going forwards. The hands did not leave me until I was quite balanced again, and they disappeared as suddenly as they came.'[6]

David made an interesting observation when he said, 'Angels tend to be shy creatures. They are messengers and so do not flaunt themselves. If at all possible they do not appear.'

Reassuring: John G. Paton (1824-1907) was a Scottish missionary to the New Hebrides. He sailed there with his newly wed wife in 1858 to begin work on Tanna, an island inhabited by savage cannibals in the South Pacific Ocean.

Having arrived in New Zealand he was deeply concerned as to how to get a ship to sail to the New Hebrides. At that time he wrote, 'I trembled, in my reduced state, at the task that seemed laid upon me again. One night, after long praying, I fell into a deep sleep in my cabin, and God granted me a Heavenly Dream or Vision which greatly comforted me ... Sweetest music, praising God, arrested me and came nearer and nearer. I gazed towards it approaching, and seemed to behold **hosts of shining beings** bursting into view ... my hand rose instinctively to shade my eyes; I cried with ecstasy ... it was a great abiding consolation. And I kept repeating to myself, "He is Lord, and they are ministering spirits; if He cheers me thus in His own work, I take courage, I know I shall succeed."'[7]

Comforting: Billy Graham records the time of his maternal grandmother's death – 'the room seemed to fill with a heavenly light' She exclaimed, '... I see angels', then 'she slumped over and was absent from the body and present with the Lord.'[8]

Vera Hudson was an elderly Christian lady, a faithful church member and dear friend. For many years she survived a nasty chest infection each winter but in her final year she

5. **Angels All Around Us – more and more people claim they've seen or felt these heavenly messengers**, Dawn Raffel, Redbook, 1992 page 82 [Cited in *Angels Among Us – Separating Fact from Fiction*, Ron Rhodes, Harvest House Publishers, USA, 1994, 2008 ISBN 978-07369-1905-0 pp. 19-20].

6. **Angels – True stories of how they touch our lives**, Hope Price, Macmillan, London, 1993 – Pan Books edition 1994 (p. 120) ISBN 0-330-32850-6.

7. **John G Paton – An Autobiography**, Hodder and Stoughton, London, 1890. (pp. 238-239).

8. **Angels – God's Secret Agents**, Billy Graham, Hodder and Stoughton, London, 1975, 1986 (p. 116). ISBN 0-340-63031-0.

was admitted to a north London Hospital. Her son and daughter had sat at her bedside comforting her throughout the day. By the late evening the nursing staff suggested that they go and have some much needed refreshments. They were only away a short time but it coincided with my pastoral visit. Clearly, Vera was very frail when I arrived. I read some familiar words of scripture to her and then gently held her hand as I prayed with her. The main light in the side room was turned off and the small over-bed lamp was dimmed. While I prayed, with my eyes closed, I sensed that a person was present with us and that there was a bright light in the room. I did not open my eyes or stop praying, thinking that whoever had come into the room would respect that I was praying with Vera. When I did open my eyes the bright light in the room had gone and to my surprise only Vera and I were in the room. I experienced an overwhelming sense of peace. I then realised that Vera was not breathing and no pulse could be detected. She was *'absent from the body and present with the Lord'* [2 Cor. 5:8]. Was it an angelic presence I sensed that night, I cannot say for certain. However, it was very real and exceedingly comforting.

SELECTIVE BIBLIOGRAPHY

All the Angels of the Bible, Herbert Lockyer, Hendrickson Publishers, Massachusetts, 7th printing 2012 (175 pages). ISBN 978-156563-198-4.

This internationally known Baptist pastor died in 1985. Thankfully his son gathered together his father's notes on the subject and supplemented with some information from his own studies to form this wonderful volume. There are valuable comments, as stated in the book title on, 'All the Angels in the Bible'.

Angels Among Us – Separating Fact from Fiction, Ron Rhodes, Harvest House Publishers, USA, 1994, 2008 (246 pages). ISBN 978-07369-1905-0.

Solid Bible facts that will help you realise what is fictitious nonsense are set out in this book by a scholarly author and broadcaster. This well-structured study has valuable footnotes and a long bibliography which will be helpful for the serious student who wants to engage in a detailed study about angels.

Angelic Beings – their Nature and Ministry, Charles D. Bell, The Religious Tract Society, London, 1875, Nabu Press, USA, 2011 (198 pages). ISBN 9781179216492.

The original publishers, the Religious Tract Society, was founded in 1799, and was a major British publisher of Christian literature intended initially for evangelism. A facsimile of this old publication was reproduced in 2011 as it was considered that the 'work is culturally important'. It is a very refreshing read on the subject.

Angels by My Side – Stories and Glimpses of these Heavenly Helpers. Betty Malz, Chosen (a division of Baker publishing Group), Minnesota USA, 1986 (121 pages). ISBN 978-080079-561-0.

Betty Malz (1929-2012) was the daughter of a minister, wife of an Assemblies of God pastor and the author of ten books. She includes some fascinating accounts and testimonies of angel assistance. Betty wants her readers to know that God's angels are still available to help.

Angels – Elect and Evil. C Fred Dickason, Moody Press, Chicago, 1975 (238 pages). ISBN 0- 8024-0222-4.

The author lectures to Christian groups on the subject of angelology. He is deeply concerned about the massive amount of interest that is being shown in angels by the occult and the false teaching that abounds about the subject. This is a well-researched helpful book that expounds the Scriptures. There is a particularly useful summary at the end of each chapter.

Angels – God's Secret Agents, Billy Graham, Hodder and Stoughton, London, 1975, 1986 (131 pages). ISBN 0-340-63031-0.

This is an easy to read 'bestseller' by a world renowned author. It is a helpful topical Bible survey with devotional applications and useful illustrative stories. A good 'starter' book to help you understand the Bible's teaching about angels.

Angels – True stories, Robert J Morgan, Thomas Nelson, USA, 2011 (142 pages) ISBN-13 978-1-4041-8975-1

This 'coffee-table' type hardback publication has several misleading images of angelic sculptured figures to enhance the ascetic appearance. However, the author is a Bible teacher devoted to *'rightly dividing'* the Word of God (2 Tim. 2:15). He reminds his readers that concerning angels, 'there is no need to be fanciful or fanatical on this subject, for the Bible provides enough solid data for satisfying our understanding'.

Angels – True stories of how they touch our lives, Hope Price, Macmillan, London, 1993 [Pan Books edition 1994] (194 pages). ISBN 0-330-32850-6.

The author is a Marie Curie nurse and the wife of an Anglican minister. It consists mostly of a collection of personal experience testimonies, including family members. There is also a short chapter giving a potted historical insight on some different thoughts held on 'The Church's View' of angels.

Angels – what the Bible teaches, Roger Ellsworth, Evangelical Press, Darlington, England, 2nd Impression (119 pages) 2007. ISBN -13 978-0-85234-617-4.

This concise little book grew out of a series of sermons preached on the topic by this Baptist pastor. It has a solid Bible base and is a very helpful introduction to this important subject. It is a 'must read' pocket size book.

Angels – Who they are and How they Help, David Jeremiah, Multnomah Books, USA,1996, 2006 (237 pages) ISBN. 978-160142-269-9.

Dr Jeremiah's fourteen clear chapter headings serve to stimulate the curious reader to learn more about the 'Agents of Heaven'. This pastor, Bible teacher and broadcaster surveys the Scriptures and uses some illustrative material of other reliable writers. He helpfully separates fact from fiction, leaving the reader in no doubt about the truth of Scripture.

Holy Angels – the Facts, Silvanus Oluoch, Tate Publishing, USA, 2009 (212 pages). ISBN 978-1-60696-632-7.

The author is a teacher, pastor, missionary and a family man. It is a specific study of God's *'holy angels'*. The book has two main parts; the second part is in the form of questions and Bible-based answers and is very profitable.

Our Friends the Angels, Irene Palmer, Elliot Stock, London, 1908. *No ISBN available.*

This now long out of print book abounds with helpful observations. Read only copies are available in the British Library and the Evangelical Library, both in London.

Spurgeon's Sermon on Angels, Charles Haddon Spurgeon, Kregal Publications, Grand Rapids, USA, 1996 (159 pages). ISBN 0-8254-3690-7.

This is a series of twelve topical sermons based both on Old and New Testament texts when the 'Prince of Preachers' was the pastor at New Park Street and the Metropolitan Tabernacle, London. C. H. Spurgeon (1834-1892) who preached his first sermon at age sixteen preached over three thousand sermons. His sermon, 'Angelic interest in the gospel' is well worth reading.

The Facts on Angels – Who they are, Where they are from and What they do, John Ankerberg & John Weldon, Harvest house Publishers, Oregon; USA, 1995 (48 pages). ISBN 1-56507-345-2.

This dual author American publication is a brief basic introduction to the subject in a question and answer format. In addition to the Bible quotations there are 176 footnote references to quotations from other publications. This is a useful slim booklet of only 48 pages but the price may well deter some.

Triumph of the Lamb – a Commentary on Revelation, Dennis E Johnson, P & R Publishing, USA, 2001 (384 pages). ISBN-13 978-0-87552-200-5.

There are more references to angels in the Book of Revelation than any other book in the Bible. For the serious Bible student it is worth having a really good commentary to assist your understanding on Revelation. This is a scholarly, but a valuable volume by a minister of the Presbyterian Church of America. Dr Johnson also serves as a professor at Westminster Theological Seminary in California.

ANSWER GUIDE

The following pages contain an Answer Guide. It is recommended that answers to the questions be attempted before turning to this guide. It is only a guide and the answers given should not be treated as exhaustive.

GUIDE TO STUDY 1

I BELIEVE IN ANGELS

DAY 1 a) God has told us the truth in the Scriptures, which are *'given by inspiration of God'* (2 Tim. 3:16). We can trust what God has told us about angels in the Bible

b) The people's willingness to listen to the teaching of God's servants and search the Scriptures for themselves every day.

c) Check the teaching to see that it is in accordance with God's Word, the Bible.

DAY 2 a) The record of the Scriptures, the testimony and experience of Christ.

b) They are rejoicing with God in heaven when a sinner repents.
They are giving help and support to Jesus at a time of great need.
They are accompanying the Lord Jesus Christ when He returns as the Judge of all the earth.

DAY 3 a) Regretfully it is possible. Many world religions and cults accept the existence of angels.

b) They taught that there is no resurrection, no angels or spirits.

DAY 4 a) No! However, we can be assured that God has revealed what He wants us to know in the Bible. There are many things that we will not fully understand in this life.

b) The Lord Jesus Christ, the Creator of all things and the Saviour of sinners.

DAY 5 a) Personal.

b) While there is no clear statement in scripture, it appears to have been prior to the creation of the visible things of the universe. The angels witnessed God's power at work in creation.

DAY 6 a) They were religious and yet they were ignorant about the *'unseen God'* who has created all things.

b) We are commanded to only worship God. In his excitement and appreciation of what John saw and heard he inappropriately bowed down to worship the angel and not just once, but twice!

DAY 7 a) It needed the Lord's intervention before Balaam could see who was causing the obstruction on the path (Num. 22:31).

b) There is a greater blessing for those who have not seen and yet have believed.

GUIDE TO STUDY 2

'A' IS FOR ANGELS

DAY 1 a) The angel Gabriel who was sent by God.
Mary was initially troubled, astonished and amazed before being calmed, reassured and submissive to God's purposes (Luke 2:38).

b) Disciples of John the Baptist. Their duty was to speak with the Lord Jesus Christ and establish that He was indeed the long awaited Lord and Saviour and to report back to John who was in prison (see Matt. 11:2).

c) *'A messenger of Satan'.* God permitted this evil spirit to be used to help His faithful servant Paul remain humble and always dependent upon His God.
The *'thorn in the flesh'* refers to an unspecified physical affliction.

DAY 2 a) The exact moment *('day and hour')* when the Lord Jesus Christ will return from heaven to earth.

b) The Apostle Paul was deeply concerned for his readers. They should not be tempted to turn away from the truth about Christ and the gospel of grace. Even if it was *'an angel from heaven'* who was preaching, they must not trust in a false way of salvation.

c) An angel was *'coming down from heaven'* (v. 1), the angel was also seen *'standing on the sea and on the land'* (v. 5) on earth.

DAY 3 a) They are sinless and holy, like the Lord Jesus Christ and they share something of His glory. They are strong and they are submissive to His word.

b) The angels in heaven are always obedient to God. However, we are all guilty of doing wrong; we have *'all sinned and fall short of the glory of God'* (Rom. 3:23) and are in need of God's forgiveness.

DAY 4 a) Abraham had a normal conversation with them, provided water for them to wash, invited them to rest and have something to eat, he seems to accept them as travellers.

b) The women were expecting to find Jesus's body lying in the tomb but were told He is risen! They needed to be reminded that Jesus had to die, just as He had told them, but that He would be raised on the third day.

c) In the case of Balaam, it required God to enable him to see the previously invisible angel who was blocking the pathway in front of him.

GUIDE TO STUDY 2 (contd)

'A' IS FOR ANGELS

DAY 5 a) Don't grow weary of worship; praise Him for His holiness, greatness and eternal nature (v. 8). Give Him *'glory and honour and thanks'* for the fact that He reigns and lives forever (v. 9). Worship with sincere humility (v. 10). Honour Him as the Eternal Creator of everything that exists (v. 11).

b) Their lives were saved and their freedom was restored so that they could continue serving their God.

DAY 6 a) First they saw an angel of the Lord and the glory of the Lord shining around (v. 9) and then *'a multitude of the heavenly host praising God'* (v. 13). They also had the joyful privilege of being told about the birth of the *'Saviour who is Christ the Lord'* (v. 11).

b) *'an innumerable company'.*

DAY 7 a) The Christian's *'living hope'*, the joy of salvation through faith in Christ, the realisation that Christ's suffering has led to glory and the gospel being preached in the power of the Holy Spirit – all these things the angels have observed but not personally experienced.

b) An individual, personally repenting, that is being sincerely sorry and turning from their sin to God.

GUIDE TO STUDY 3

WHO'S WHO AMONG THE ANGELS?

DAY 1 a) Those who believe on the Lord Jesus Christ shall not perish eternally but have everlasting life.
Those who do not believe are condemned already, they love darkness and they are practicing evil.

b) They will have to suffer God's fearful judgement.

DAY 2 a) The great dragon, the serpent called the Devil and Satan.

b) Michael, the archangel (the first or chief amongst the angels).

DAY 3 a) God had the first created man, Adam, name them.

b) God (not the angels).

c) Singing in a *'loud voice'* and worshipping God – *'who sits on the throne'* and Jesus Christ – *'The Lamb' 'who lives forever and ever'.*

DAY 4 a) *'To guard the way to the tree of life'* – to stop sinful Adam and Eve taking the fruit.

b) Personal – perhaps the presence of God's glory (v. 4); the loud sound (v. 5) their unusual appearance or their association with the Temple of God (the Lord's House).

DAY 5 a) God's holiness and glory.
They touched Isaiah's mouth with the live coal and pronounced that his sin was taken away.

b) Six. (Many artist's pictures usually portray angelic beings with two wings).

c) We never read of Cherubim speaking but the Seraphim seen by Isaiah did.

DAY 6 a) Godly men, humans. There is no procreation amongst angels (Mark 12:25).

b) Angels in heaven.

c) Christians, those who have believed on the Lord Jesus Christ.

DAY 7 a) Personal – perhaps thankful, very grateful and reassured.

b) Personal – O.T. examples: Lot and his family (Gen. 19:15); Daniel (Dan. 6:22).
N.T. examples: Jesus, Joseph and Mary (Matt. 2:13); Peter (Acts 12:7-11).

GUIDE TO STUDY 4

FEATURES OF ANGELS WHO HAVE FALLEN

DAY 1 a) To be exalted and be like Almighty God (*'the Most High'*).

b) The opposite of what Lucifer strived for, he was brought down.

c) Ensure that unconfessed *'iniquity'* is not found in us, that our heart is not lifted up in pride.

DAY 2 a) Satan *('the serpent')* lured Adam and Eve into disobeying God and subsequently we are all born with a sinful nature.

b) *'Satan entered Judas'* and he betrayed Christ. Satan had requested to test *('sift')* Peter but Jesus had prayed for him and even though he fell he was restored and served the Saviour.

DAY 3 a) Personal – perhaps Satan was deliberately tempting Jesus when He was alone and hungry. How Satan misused the Scriptures. Satan was offering Jesus *'the kingdoms of the world and their glory'* – they did not belong to Satan.

b) He quoted from scripture each time, from the Book of Deuteronomy.

c) Jesus knew that He *'must suffer ... be killed, and after three days rise again'.* Not wanting God's plan of salvation to succeed, Satan prompted Peter to wrongly rebuke the Saviour.

DAY 4 a) Questioning the validity of God's commands and causing Eve to doubt God's word.

b) Satan (the enemy) *'snatches away'* the seed of God's word from the hearts of people.
Satan actively seeks to disrupt God's work by sowing his seed where the good seed of God's Word has been sown already.

c) Possibly because he wanted to impede the Apostle Paul's preaching and teaching ministry.

DAY 5 a) Be self-controlled, watchful, resist the Devil, standing firm in faith.

b) In our human weakness we need the Lord's strength and power together with the protection of the whole armour of God. We are fighting against evil spiritual forces (Eph. 6:12).

c) Personal – perhaps to encourage submission to God and to instil confidence to resist the Devil.

GUIDE TO STUDY 4 (contd)

FEATURES OF ANGELS WHO HAVE FALLEN

DAY 6 a) Knowing about Jesus will not make us a child of God. We need to love Christ (John 8:42) and listen to the truth of what God says in His Word (John 8:47).

b) Satan (Acts 5:3). The sudden death of Ananias and his wife Sapphira.

DAY 7 a) They are fully aware of who Jesus is. That they are the exact opposite of all that Jesus is. They are mindful that they are destined for destruction. They know Jesus is the *'Holy One of God'* and that He has authority over them.

b) A crushing blow was brought against Satan when Christ was crucified, *'lifted up'* (John 12:32).

GUIDE TO STUDY 5

THE SAVIOUR'S SUPREMACY OVER ANGELS

DAY 1 a) The confused crowds had a variety of opinions that included: John the Baptist, Elijah, or even a resurrected prophet! Peter emphatically said that Jesus is, *'The Christ of God'.*

b) (Luke 22) Christ was aware of their obstinate unbelief (v. 67), their unwillingness to release Him (v. 68), His imminent exaltation (v. 69) and the fact that He is 'the Son of God'.

c) The Lord addressed her personally – *'Jesus said to her, Mary!'*

DAY 2 a) He purged (cleansed) sin – by His death on the cross.

b) The angels are inferior to the Lord Jesus Christ.

c) To sit with Christ on His throne – reign with Him.

DAY 3 a) The name Jesus means Saviour – *'He will save His people from their sins'* (Matt. 1:21)

b) Christ is superior, *'so much better than the angels'.*

c) Because God (the Father) *'has highly exalted Him'.*

DAY 4 a) The Son is a powerful King with authority who will triumph over all and the angels are His (Ps. 104:4).

b) Psalm 2:7 and 2 Samuel 7:14 (Heb. 1:5).
Psalm 104:4 (Heb. 1:7).

DAY 5 a) God has authority to do so as the Divine Creator of all things.

b) Worship God.

c) Not to worship the angel but to *'Worship God'.*

DAY 6 a) Christ is divine, he has authority, he reigns as King.

b) Personal – perhaps reassured as God's characteristics such as faithfulness, love, mercy and grace remain unchanged.

DAY 7 a) God created and crowned mankind with *'glory and honour'* – made us in His image, unlike any of the other creatures God made. God granted humans the authority *'to have dominion'* over the animals.

b) God the Father sent His Son into the world and then enthroned Him as King.

GUIDE TO STUDY 6

ANGELIC APPEARANCES AND APPOINTMENTS

DAY 1 a) The total destruction of the evil cities would take place the very next day.

b) They pulled Lot into the house and struck the evil men with blindness. They told Lot to leave the city with his family and the angels led them out of the city.

c) Christ was warning about His return and that judgement would be sudden and unexpected.

DAY 2 a) Abraham was able to return with his son Isaac alive.

God kept His promise about Abraham's descendants and *'all the nations of the earth'* be blessed.

b) Personal – perhaps the perfect timing, not a second too late!

DAY 3 a) God had called, led him and made a remarkable promise to him.

b) He prayed asking that God would grant him success in his assignment and to reveal God's will to him.

DAY 4 a) He admitted his own sin, questioned God's punishment of the people and requested that God's judgment be directed to himself and his family.

b) Construct an altar to the Lord so that offerings could be made on it.

c) He disciplines (chastens) and rebukes.

DAY 5 a) Jezebel had sent messengers to Elijah threatening to kill him by the next day.

b) He was given strength to make the long journey of forty days to Mount Horeb.

c) If we are able to do so, we are to work in order to eat.

DAY 6 a) God's holiness and the fact that His glory fills the whole earth.

b) To touch Isaiah's lips with the coal from the altar. Then they reassured him that his iniquity was removed and his sin atoned for.

c) God requires that those who serve Him are cleansed from sin. Without holiness we will not see the Lord, we will not be granted admission to heaven.

DAY 7 a) The king said to Daniel, *'Your God, whom you serve continually, He will deliver you'* (v. 16).

b) *'My God sent His angel and shut the lions' mouths ...'* (v. 22). He'd been found innocent in God's sight.

c) His faith in the Lord – *'he believed in his God'.*

GUIDE TO STUDY 7

THE ANGEL WHO IS MIGHTY

DAY 1 a) God was concerned for Hagar, He took the initiative and sought her in her distress.

b) Hagar identifies *'the Angel of the LORD'* as God – *'You are the God Who Sees'* (Gen. 16:13).

DAY 2 a) Jacob was told, *'you have struggled with God …'* (v. 28).
Jacob naming the location, *'Peniel: For I have seen God face to face …'* (v. 30).

b) The disability was a reminder to humbly submit to the Lord.

c) God's servants, those who love and serve Christ.

DAY 3 a) He was a shepherd and then the leader of God's people, their human deliverer.

b) The suffering and oppression of the children of Israel.

DAY 4 a) The mouth of Balaam's donkey (Num. 22:28) and Balaam's eyes (Num. 22:31).

b) While Balaam admitted he had done wrong he never expressed sorrow for his sin or ask for God's forgiveness. God holds us responsible to both admit our guilt and request His forgiveness.

c) It is possible to be religious and speak for the Lord and yet not be a true Believer.

DAY 5 a) Joshua was told, *'take your sandal off your foot …'*

b) It was a formidable and daunting task and they had to exercise faith in God.

DAY 6 a) Nine/Ten times, depending on the Bible translation used (vv. 3; 13; 15; 16 twice; 17; (18); 20; 21 twice).
'A Man of God … His countenance was like the countenance of the Angel of God, very awesome'.

b) Because they had seen *'God'* (v. 22).

DAY 7 a) Elijah immediately obeyed.

b) What he prophesied came to pass and the king died.

c) The eleven disciples of Christ.

GUIDE TO STUDY 8

THE SAVIOUR'S ASSOCIATION WITH ANGELS

DAY 1 a) An *'angel of the Lord'* (Luke 1:11). The angel is named *'Gabriel'* (Luke 1:26). He normally dwells in God's presence and he was sent to share good news. He is sympathetic and reassuring. He is able to predict future events.

b) The Lord Jesus Christ

c) God often sends His angels to comfort and reassure His people.

DAY 2 a) He had no human companionship, he was hungry and was probably feeling spiritually drained after His demanding ordeal amongst wild beasts and with Satan.

b) By praying, in the sure knowledge that Christ will *'sympathise with our weakness'.*

DAY 3 a) Angels do not marry, there is no pro-creation amongst them, neither do they die.

b) Angels, at Christ's command, will assist the Lord to *'separate the wicked from among the just'.*

c) If we love the Lord and seek to do His will, we can be assured that there are a multitude of angels that God could possibly use for our good.

DAY 4 a) Peter had said that he did not want Jesus to die and rise again as predicted by the Lord.
Peter had become an offence and a stumbling block to Christ doing the will of God the Father.

b) An angel.

c) Christ's suffering on the cross predicted by the prophets, and the subsequent glories of His kingdom.

DAY 5 a) The guards were terrified.
The women were reassured, obeyed the instruction to tell the Disciples of Christ's resurrection and left the grave with reverential fear and joy.

b) They *'did not believe'* what they were told (Luke 24:11)

DAY 6 a) Jesus will return, in a similar way.

b) Christ is in Heaven, at the right hand of God the Father, and the angels are subject to Him.

DAY 7 a) *'all the holy angels'* (Matt. 25:31).

b) Personal.

c) Christians are further reassured of Christ's return. Those Believers who have died and those who are alive, will be raised to meet the Lord and be with Him forever.

GUIDE TO STUDY 9

AMAZING ACCOMPLISHMENTS

DAY 1 a) They were able to go to the temple and teach and also speak to their persecutors about Christ.

b) They will suffer tribulation. They are to be of good cheer, as Christ has overcome the world.

c) Suffering persecution.

DAY 2 a) Those who have become *'disciples'* of Christ from *'all the nations'.*

b) Christ's disciples would be empowered by the Holy Spirit.
They were to be His Worldwide witnesses.

c) Philip explained the scripture passage being read by the eunuch.
Philip confirmed that the eunuch believed in Christ with all his heart, and then he baptised him.

DAY 3 a) An *'angel of God'* may appear in a vision with an important personal message (Acts 10:3).
Having delivered the message the angel did not remain but departed (Acts 10:7).
An angel can appear as a man *'in bright clothing'* (Acts 10:30).
The angel was *'standing'* (Acts 11:13) – not hovering or flying!

b) He fell down at Peter's feet in reverence (Acts 10:25-26).

DAY 4 a) Herod was harassing the church, having killed James and sought to please the Jews.
Peter was imprisoned waiting execution.

b) Herod was about to bring Peter out of prison in the hope of having him executed like James.

c) When they are *'reproached for the name of Christ'.*

DAY 5 a) Personal – perhaps the suddenness and fatality of the angel's intervention

b) An enemy of the Church was removed and *'the word of God grew and multiplied'.*

c) A fall.

DAY 6 a) The resurrection of the dead and the existence of angels or spirits.

b) Personal – perhaps because without the resurrection Christ would still be in the grave and we would be without hope.
God created the angels who frequently help God's people in times of great need.
Both of these matters are stated as fact in the Bible and we should believe them.

GUIDE TO STUDY 9 (contd)

AMAZING ACCOMPLISHMENTS

DAY 7 a) While on route to stand trial before Caesar, he was in great danger, caught in the midst of a furious storm and was about to be shipwrecked.

b) Paul was reassured that he would get to speak to Caesar, and he was able to console all aboard the ship.

GUIDE TO STUDY 10

THE ANGELS' FINAL AWESOME ACTIVITIES

DAY 1 a) Worship, praise and adoration.

b) Christ *('the Lamb')* and God.

c) There were those who have been redeemed *'out of every tribe and tongue and people and nation'* singing the song.

DAY 2 a) He wept, probably out of concern and disappointment that initially no one was found worthy of the task. Then one of the elders informed him of the power and authority of Christ *('the Lion of the tribe of Judah …')*.

b) Personal – perhaps appalled and disgusted by her revolting character and dreadful deeds.

DAY 3 a) That everyone on earth should respect the Lord, give Him glory and worship their Creator.
The worshippers of *'the beast'* will suffer the most terrible judgement in the presence of the holy angels and Christ.

b) God longs for people to turn from evil and trust in Him so as to avoid His judgement.

DAY 4 a) Perhaps to ensure that the whole earth is protected (*'four corners of the earth'* – north, south, east and west).

b) The Lord Himself *'surrounds His people'*.
Believers cannot be snatched from Christ's or God the Father's hand.

DAY 5 a) Angels (Seven).
On those who are associated with the *'beast'*, the Devil. That is those who are not God's people.

b) Personal – perhaps a 'blessed assurance' of sins forgiven because of God's mercy and reassuring promises.

DAY 6 a) God's judgement of the *'great harlot'* and the *'marriage/wedding supper of the Lamb'*.

b) Personal – perhaps when our circumstances are difficult and if we do not focus on the Lord.

DAY 7 a) He fell down to worship the angel. It's only God who is to be worshipped.

b) The statements of Scripture. The long standing promises of Christ, and the message of the angels at Christ's ascension.

GUIDE TO STUDY 11

THE ASSISTANCE OF THE ANGELS

DAY 1 a) Personal – have read about or known someone - relating to the protection of angels [Ps. 91:11].

b) Personal – perhaps thrilled by the way God preserved the life of His servant, thus permitting him to continue his ministry amongst such a needy group of people.

c) Personal – perhaps appreciative for the repeated reassurance of God's help for those who love Him, especially during times of trouble.

DAY 2 a) Those who *'fear'* the Lord, that is all who respect, honour and trust Him.

b) *'God sent His angel and shut the lions' mouths …'*

c) They were both convinced that God's angel protected and delivered them from danger.

DAY 3 a) They *'cried to the LORD'* for help and God answered their prayer. They valued God's word.

b) Personal – perhaps they would feel deprived of God's truth with its promises and directives.
It would be a time of spiritual famine (Amos 8:11).

DAY 4 a) Angels

b) Family members were in danger of losing their lives.

c) God promises to guide us and charges us not to be obstinate like ignorant farm creatures.

DAY 5 a) Personal – perhaps thankful reassurance, comforted by God's promises and watch over us.

b) The LORD only opened the eyes of Elisha's servant after he had prayed for the young man.
Balaam did not see the Angel of the LORD at first it needed the Lord to open his eyes.

DAY 6 a) An angel of God stood by him reassuring him that he and all aboard the ship would reach their destination.

b) God's holy angels who serve the Lord and His people.
The experience reassured John Paton that the Lord would grant him success in his service for Christ.

GUIDE TO STUDY 11 (contd)

THE ASSISTANCE OF THE ANGELS

DAY 7 a) Lazarus was carried by angels to heaven *('Abraham's bosom').*
The rich man was buried and his soul was tormented in hell without any hope of relief.

b) The Lord may be pleased to grant us the help of angels. The Believer's death is precious in God's sight. Christ has prepared a place in heaven for those who trust in Him. Christ will return and all those who have trusted the Saviour will be with Him.